Helion & Company Limited
Unit 8 Amherst Business Centre
Budbrooke Road
Warwick
CV34 5WE
England
Tel. 01926 499 619
Email: info@helion.co.uk
Website: www.helion.co.uk
Twitter: @helionbooks
Visit our blog http://blog.helion.co.uk/

Designed and typeset by Farr out Publications, Wokingham, Berkshire
Cover design Paul Hewitt, Battlefield Design (www.battlefield-design.co.uk)

ISBN 978-1-804513-66-8

British Library Cataloguing-in-Publication Data
A catalogue record for this book is available from the British Library

We always welcome receiving book proposals from prospective authors.

CONTENTS

MAP OF EUROPE 1945–1992

Note: In order to simplify the use of this book, all names, locations and geographic designations are as provided in *The Times World Atlas*, or other traditionally accepted major sources of reference, as of the time of described events.

ABBREVIATIONS

AM	Academia Militar (Military Academy)
ANP	Acção Nacional Popular (National Popular Action)
CCE	Comissão Coordenadora Executiva (Executive Coordinating Commission)
CCFAG	Comando-Chefe das Forças Armadas da Guiné (Commander-in-Chief of the Armed Forces in Guinea)
CEME	Chefe do Estado-Maior do Exército (Chief of Staff of the Army)
CEMGFA	Chefe do Estado-Maior General das Forças Armadas (Chief of Staff of the Armed Forces)
CIOE	Centro de Instrução de Operações Especiais (Special Operations Training Centre)
CSDN	Conselho Superior de Defesa Nacional (Higher Council of National Defence)
CSM	Conselho Superior Militar (Higher Military Council)
ECS	Escola Central de Sargentos (Sergeants Central School)
EME	Estado-Maior do Exército (Army Staff)
EMGFA	Estado-Maior General das Forças Armadas (Armed Forces General Staff)
EPA	Escola Prática de Artilharia (Artillery Practical School)
EPC	Escola Prática de Cavalaria (Cavalry Practical School)
EPI	Escola Prática de Infantaria (Infantry Practical School)
FA	Forças Armadas (Armed Forces)
FAP	Força Aérea Portuguesa (Portuguese Air Force)
FNLA	Frente Nacional de Libertação de Angola (National Front for the Liberation of Angola)
FRELIMO	Frente de Libertação de Moçambique (Mozambique Liberation Front)
GE	Grupos Especiais (Special Groups)
MFA	Movimento das Forças Armadas (Armed Forces Movement)
MPLA	Movimento Popular de Libertação de Angola (Popular Movement for the Liberation of Angola)
PAIGC	Partido Africano da Independência da Guiné e Cabo Verde (African Party for the Independence of Guinea and Cape Verde)
PIDE/DGS	Polícia Internacional e de Defesa do Estado/ Direcção Geral de Segurança (International and State Defence Police/Directorate-General for Security)
QP	Quadro Permanente (Permanent Staff)
RC	Regimento de Cavalaria (Regiment of Cavalry)
RTP	Radio Televisão Portuguesa (Radio Television Portugal)
SGDN	Secretariado-Geral da Defesa Nacional (General Secretariat of National Defence)
TO	Teatro de Operações (Theatres of Operations)
UNITA	União Nacional para a Independência Total de Angola (National Union for the Total Independence of Angola)
UPA	União das Populações de Angola (Union of the Populations of Angola)
VICE-CEMGFA	Vice-Chefe do Estado-Maior General das Forças Armadas (Vice-Chief of Staff of the Armed Forces)
ZACVG	Zona Aérea de Cabo Verde e Guiné (Air Zone of Cape Verde and Guinea)

PREFACE

To elaborate this work, the authors resorted mainly to archival research, having consulted the most relevant Portuguese archives, in addition to the archives of the French Ministry of Foreign Affairs and the American National Archives in Washington D.C. We also used the newspapers of the time as sources of information and the memories of the main protagonists of this period, from the President of the Council to the President of the Republic, ministers, secretaries of state, diplomats, members of parliament and military personnel. The authors would also like to thank Miguel Caetano, Luís Campos e Cunha and Luís Costa Correia for their personal testimonies, which allowed us to clarify some doubts. Finally, a special thanks to Orlando Pereira for reviewing the manuscript and providing helpful suggestions.

José Matos and Zélia Oliveira
October 2023

INTRODUCTION

On 25 April 1974, a movement of young captains brought down, with practically no resistance, the dictatorial regime that had been in power for over 40 years in Portugal. In the early hours of that day, a military movement unleashed a series of operations that, in less than 24 hours, defeated the forces loyal to the regime, neutralising any possibility of reaction. Few forces resisted the insurgents and the only resistance worthy of note came from the political police who, in the heat of the revolution, opened fire on the surrounding

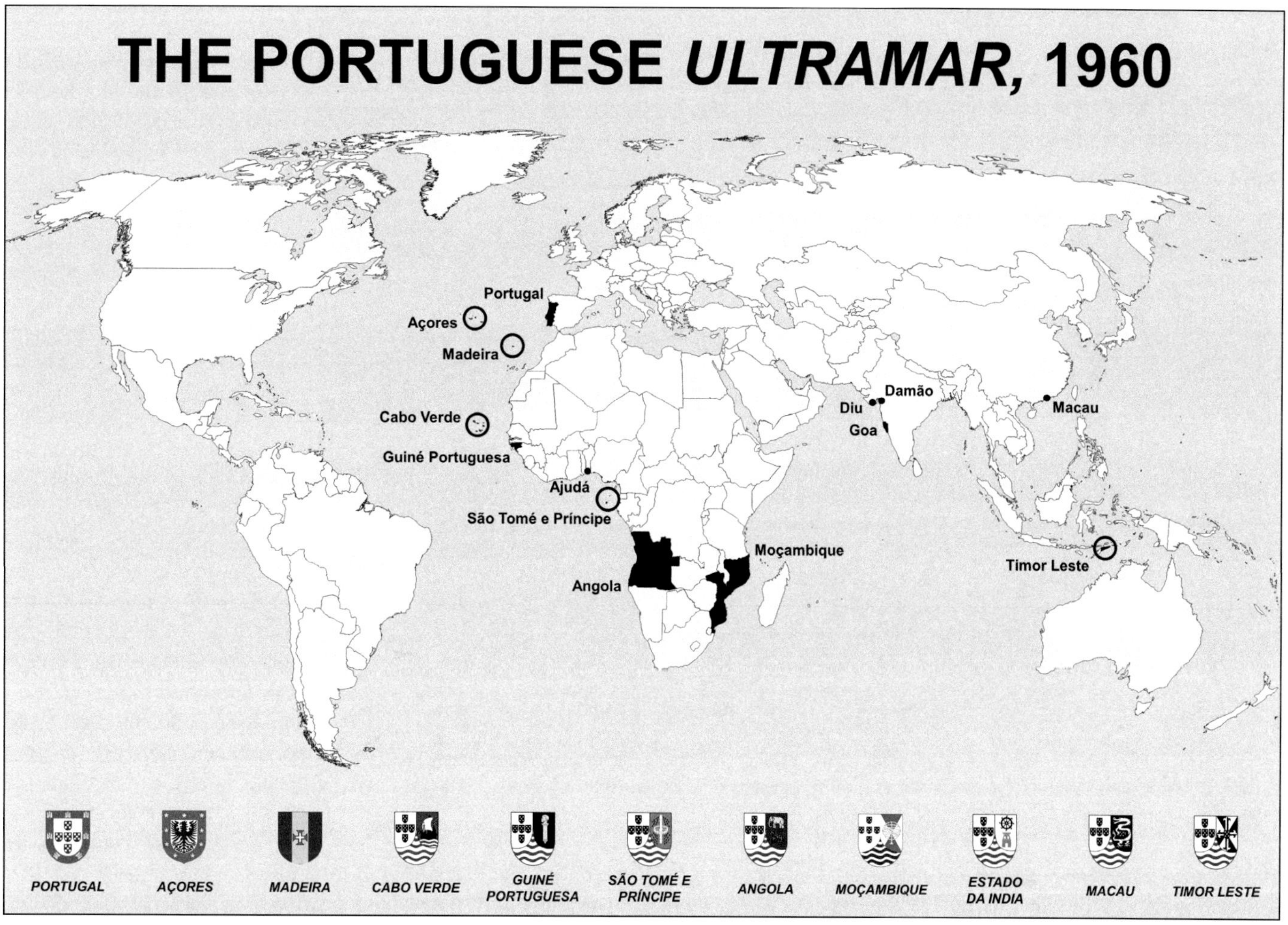

The Portuguese overseas empire in 1960, when Portugal had possessions on three continents. (Matthew M. Hurley)

crowd causing four deaths. In the streets of Lisbon, the people enthusiastically joined the military revolt and started offering food, drinks, and red carnations to the soldiers, who decided to stick them in the barrels of their rifles, making the revolt become known as the Carnation Revolution. Although it began with a military coup d'état, the 25th of April paved the way for democracy, and there is no comparison to other similar revolutions. It was also a unique event in the European context of the time that broke Portugal's isolation and brought it closer to other Western democracies.

The Portuguese dictatorship had begun in 1933 with António de Oliveira Salazar and the foundation of the so-called Estado Novo. Salazar ruled the country until 1968, when he had to leave power due to illness. The old dictator had not designated a successor, which led the President of the Republic, Admiral Américo Thomaz, to choose someone to replace Salazar. Thomaz eventually chose Marcello Caetano, one of the most prominent figures of the Estado Novo, who had been a minister under Salazar in the 1940s and 1950s and was seen as the strongest candidate to succeed the dictator. The new president of the Council of Ministers took over the executive in September 1968 and received as his inheritance, a war in the Portuguese territories in Africa that was consuming more and more of the nation's resources. The war had started in Angola in 1961, but afterwards, had also broken out in Guinea and Mozambique, and Portugal insisted on keeping its African possessions, facing the guerrilla forces that tried to expel the Portuguese.

However, the prolongation of the war started to create difficulties for the regime, which began to lack career officers to command the troops in Africa. The problem led the Minister of Defence and of the Army, Viana Rebelo, to try to facilitate the access of militia officers (who were not career officers) to the permanent staff, which caused great discontent among career officers, who felt discredited by the measure. This special access regime had been created in July 1973 and allowed militia officers to move into the permanent cadre by attending an intensive course at the Military Academy, for two consecutive semesters, followed by six months of service at a practical school; this contrasted with the training of officers at the Academy, which lasted four years. There was also the problem that new officers could overtake some career officers in the seniority list. The minister still tried to solve the problem by issuing a corrective decree in August of that year, but the damage was already done.

The problem of professional prestige began to be raised by career officers who felt their status was in question, especially junior officers, who were the most affected by the competition.[1] From then on, a growing mobilisation of these officers who wanted the controversial decrees to be revoked, was witnessed. The protest came to the knowledge of the President of the Council (Prime Minister) Marcello Caetano in September 1973, through a written statement signed by officers of the permanent staff serving in Guinea and others would follow. The warnings also came from the Chief of Staff of the Armed Forces (CEMGFA) himself, General Costa Gomes, who alerted Marcello Caetano to the dissatisfaction present in the military forces and to which a satisfactory response needed to be given. However, Caetano refused to act under pressure from the protesters, although he eventually gave in to the demands – against his will – by revoking the diplomas and increasing the military salaries at the end of the year.[2]

However, by this time, the movement was already unstoppable and would gain additional motivation in 1974 with the publication

Parade of Portuguese troops in Luanda in 1961 when war broke out in the north of the colony. (Manuel da Graça collection)

of the book, *Portugal e o Futuro* (Portugal and the Future) by General António Spínola, Vice-Chief of Staff of the Armed Forces (Vice-CEMGFA), which proclaimed the impossibility of a military victory in the war being waged in the Portuguese colonies. Spínola had been governor and military commander of Guinea and was convinced that any military solution to the conflict in Africa was impossible and that the only solution would be to create a federation between Portugal and the colonies, with the African territories also becoming states within this new organisational scheme.[3] Marcello Caetano was clearly surprised by the content of the first part of the book, whose publication had been authorised by the CEMGFA, Costa Gomes, and he saw Spínola's work as an attack on the government's policy and made the two generals aware of this. At a meeting he had at his home in Lisbon with the two officers on 22 February 1974, he even told them that he saw the book as a manifesto to promote a military coup d'état.[4]

The divorce between the head of government and the highest representatives of the Armed Forces was thus declared. Feeling undermined by the attitude of the two generals, Caetano suggested to the President of the Republic, Américo Thomaz, that he accept the resignation of the executive. As his request was not accepted, he rehearsed the first of a series of 'stunts' or 'leaks': a speech on 5 March in the National Assembly in favour of the intransigent defence of Overseas Territories or, in other words, the continuation of the war. Precisely on this day, the captains' movement took a decisive step when it recognised at a meeting in Cascais, near Lisbon, attended by around 200 officers, that Portugal's main problem was the war in Africa and that this required a political and not a military solution, a solution which could involve the independence of the African peoples.[5]

On 14 March, Marcello tried to compromise the Armed Forces with the government's overseas policy by promoting in his official residence, a ceremony with all general officers in active service, to express their agreement with the government's policy. Costa Gomes and António Spínola refused to attend and were dismissed the following day.

The regime's dismissal of the two generals aggravated the discontent that existed in the movement of the captains, and some attempted a coup d'état by rising up the Regiment of Infantry 5 from Caldas da Rainha, 90km north of Lisbon, which on 16 March, left for the capital to overthrow the government.[6] This was an isolated attack without the support of other military units and was neutralised by forces loyal to the regime. The insurgents were arrested, but the coup attempt from Caldas was not useless. The way it was unleashed and the reaction of government forces, allowed Otelo Saraiva de Carvalho, the strategist of the 25th of April, to realise that there was no organised plan to confront the movement.[7] Salgueiro Maia, another leading figure of the revolution, would later say that 'the uprising (of 25 April) was done if only to free the comrades of Caldas da Rainha.'[8] In short, from 16 March onwards, the starting signal for the April Revolution was given.

It is clear that Marcello Caetano sensed that the end was near, yet he tried to maintain the course set in 1968, when he became head of the executive, in the hope that the military would not rebel against the regime. In the 1969 election campaign for the National Assembly, he had defended the 'progressive development and growing autonomy' of the Overseas Territories, but it was clear that this autonomy did not mean immediate independence, nor did it mean reaching agreements with the liberation movements.

For Caetano, the question of autonomy essentially involved the revision of the organic law for Overseas Territories, which came into effect in 1972 and allowed greater participation and representation of native elements in the colonial administration, as well as greater powers for local organs in the colonies.[9] It is likely that in his mind, the possibility of a future independence was not completely ruled out, but it would be a slow process that would take time to form a multiracial society in which the interests of the white minority were assured and that did not go through negotiations with African nationalist movements.[10] However, Caetano's strategy had a major problem which was Guinea.

The military situation in the small African colony was quite unfavourable to the Portuguese troops and tended to get worse. According to Otelo Saraiva de Carvalho, in Guinea, until March 1973, there was no risk of military defeat. The situation changed drastically with the arrival of the first Strela surface-to-air missiles in the hands of the guerrillas, supplied by Moscow. The first Portuguese fighters (two Fiat G.91) were shot down at the end of March 1973 in the south of Guinea and the fear of military defeat rose, since aviation was the great advantage that the Portuguese troops had in

Former Premier António Salazar, centre, is greeted by unidentified supporters during a rare public appearance after voting in the 1969 elections. Clearly ill, Salazar had given way to Marcello Caetano, who was younger and more liberal but followed the same policy in Africa. (AP)

Marcello Caetano taking office on 27 September 1968. At the time, there was a great expectation that Caetano could reform the regime and solve the problem of Africa. But Salazar's successor was not able to solve the nation's most pressing problem: the Overseas war. (Lisbon Archive of Photography/Portuguese Centre of Photography)

that territory. Otelo describes how the situation was tense in Bissau and that the regime in Lisbon could blame the military for the defeat in Guinea, as had already happened in 1961, when Portugal lost Goa, Damão and Diu to India.[11]

The defeat in India had been a traumatic event and the military had not forgotten it but Caetano did not want to abandon Guinea before the Portuguese had left Angola and Mozambique. For him, Guinea was part of the whole and could not be treated independently from the other colonies, since if he left Guinea, he would run the risk of having to do the same in Angola and Mozambique.[12] He explained this to Spínola in a letter in February 1973, where the problem was quite clear: 'there cannot be a policy for Guinea that is different from the one followed or planned for the whole overseas territory.'[13] Caetano was adamant on the Guinea issue, showing that he had no medium-term solutions for the war and that the military had to continue to fight for Portuguese permanence in Africa, something that made less and less sense in the minds of the Portuguese troops.

It is in this atmosphere of uncertainty and dissatisfaction regarding the continuation of the war that the captains' movement began to germinate and Spínola decided to publish his book so that the country 'would awake from the lethargic sleep into which the great mass of the Portuguese had fallen.'[14]

In early 1974, Portugal began to feel pressure from some European allies to solve the Guinea problem, where the guerrillas had already declared the territory's independence in 1973, trying to force international recognition. Many Western countries had not recognised this independence, but it was obvious that Portugal was in an increasingly difficult situation in the international context and some European allies were trying to help. This was the case for France, which during the visit of the Portuguese Minister of Foreign Affairs, Rui Patrício, to the country in January 1974, made it felt that help was available to find a negotiated solution for Guinea.[15] The same happened in England, which developed contacts to provide a secret meeting in London between a Portuguese representative and members of the Guinean guerrillas.[16]

Taking advantage of the interest of the French in the Guinea question, Pedro Feytor Pinto, who worked in the Secretariat of State for Information and Tourism, went to Paris at the beginning of April. He went to meet Jacques Foccart, President Pompidou's advisor for African affairs, and Jean Mourichaud-Beaupré, who had been ambassador to some African countries, in order to seek the support of more moderate African political leaders, such as Senghor in Senegal or Houphouet-Boigny in Ivory Coast. He hoped they would help the Portuguese in a solution of progressive autonomy that would avoid the negative effects of a sudden independence but the French, who were well informed about the internal situation in the country, were quite clear about the future of the regime: Portugal had 'a government with a suspended sentence.'[17] They were indeed right. The regime established by Salazar four decades earlier was about to fall by the hand of the military.

1
PORTUGAL AND THE FUTURE

A rebel army on patrol armed with some of the issued range of Russian weapons during the Portuguese Colonial War, Guinea-Bissau, West Africa. (Reg Lancaster/Express/Hulton Archive/Getty Images)

Marcello Caetano in Guinea in April 1969. During his visit at that time to the three colonies, Caetano was convinced that he could not abandon the Portuguese living in these territories.(Diário de Notícias)

On the afternoon of 15 February 1974, Marcello Caetano presided over the last meeting of the Higher Council of National Defence (CSDN). Gathered at the official residence of the Council's president, the ministers of Defence, Finance, Interior, Foreign Affairs, Navy, Army, and Overseas Territories, as well as the Secretary of State for Aeronautics and the Chief of Staff of the Armed Forces (CEMGFA), discussed the war in Africa and the government's efforts to maintain the colonies.[1] Unlike his predecessor, António de Oliveira Salazar, Caetano frequently convened this consultative council, although he felt it was too formal and time-consuming, with useless discussions and no practical results.[2] However, the CSDN allowed Caetano to be informed about the development of the war in the Overseas Territories. From the information he received, the President of the Council knew what was happening on the three war fronts and where the guerrillas were strongest in fighting the Portuguese troops. The war had been on-going for 13 years and Caetano easily realised the difficulty of fighting well-armed and motivated guerrillas in the struggle for independence. However, in his spirit, he was convinced that he could not give up, that he could not abandon the Portuguese living in Africa.

The meeting began with the CEMGFA, General Costa Gomes, explaining the evolution of the military situation in Guinea, which was serious due to the fact that the Portuguese forces were facing a heavily armed guerrilla force with access to sophisticated combat means.

Costa Gomes informed those present that a contract had been signed for the acquisition of a battery of anti-aircraft missiles to defend Bissau. In addition, the government was quickly seeking to acquire anti-tank weapons to confront the armoured vehicles said to be in the possession of the PAIGC (African Party for the Independence of Guinea and Cape Verde) on Guinea's southern border. The casualties caused by the guerrillas to the Portuguese forces in Guinea in 1973 were 347 dead and 1007 wounded – a very high number. In Guinea, the number of casualties per combat was higher than in Mozambique or Angola, which showed the gravity of the situation.[3]

The Crotale missile system, which Portugal even bought in 1974 from the French. The system arrived too late to be used in the war. (Thomson-CSF)

Costa Gomes also highlighted what was happening in Mozambique with the deterioration of the internal situation in the colony due to political, economic, and social factors. On the social issue, Costa Gomes drew attention to the segregation that existed between the various layers of the population, which made it easier for the guerrillas and even some of the white population, to entice the black population. Costa Gomes regretted that structures and plans created several years ago to mitigate the problem of segregation, had been forgotten. He also criticised the military strategy that had been followed by the previous commander-in-chief, Kaúlza de Arriaga, with which he disagreed and, in his opinion, proved to be completely wrong. At this level, he stressed that the lower-echelon military commands themselves did not identify with the strategy being followed, and that it was necessary to make changes in the counter-subversion strategy, as well as changes in the territorial command structure.

At this point of the meeting, Marcello Caetano intervened to mention that the government was experiencing great difficulties in buying arms on the international markets, giving, as an example, the case of the French Crotale anti-aircraft missiles, which had required a major diplomatic operation.[4] The French government had agreed to sell the missiles for 75 million francs on the understanding that they were defensive weapons and would not be used to fight guerrillas.[5]

Another problem that needed urgent resolution was the defence of the Cabora-Bassa reservoir on the Zambezi River. The Minister of the Navy, Pereira Crespo, complained about the captivation of

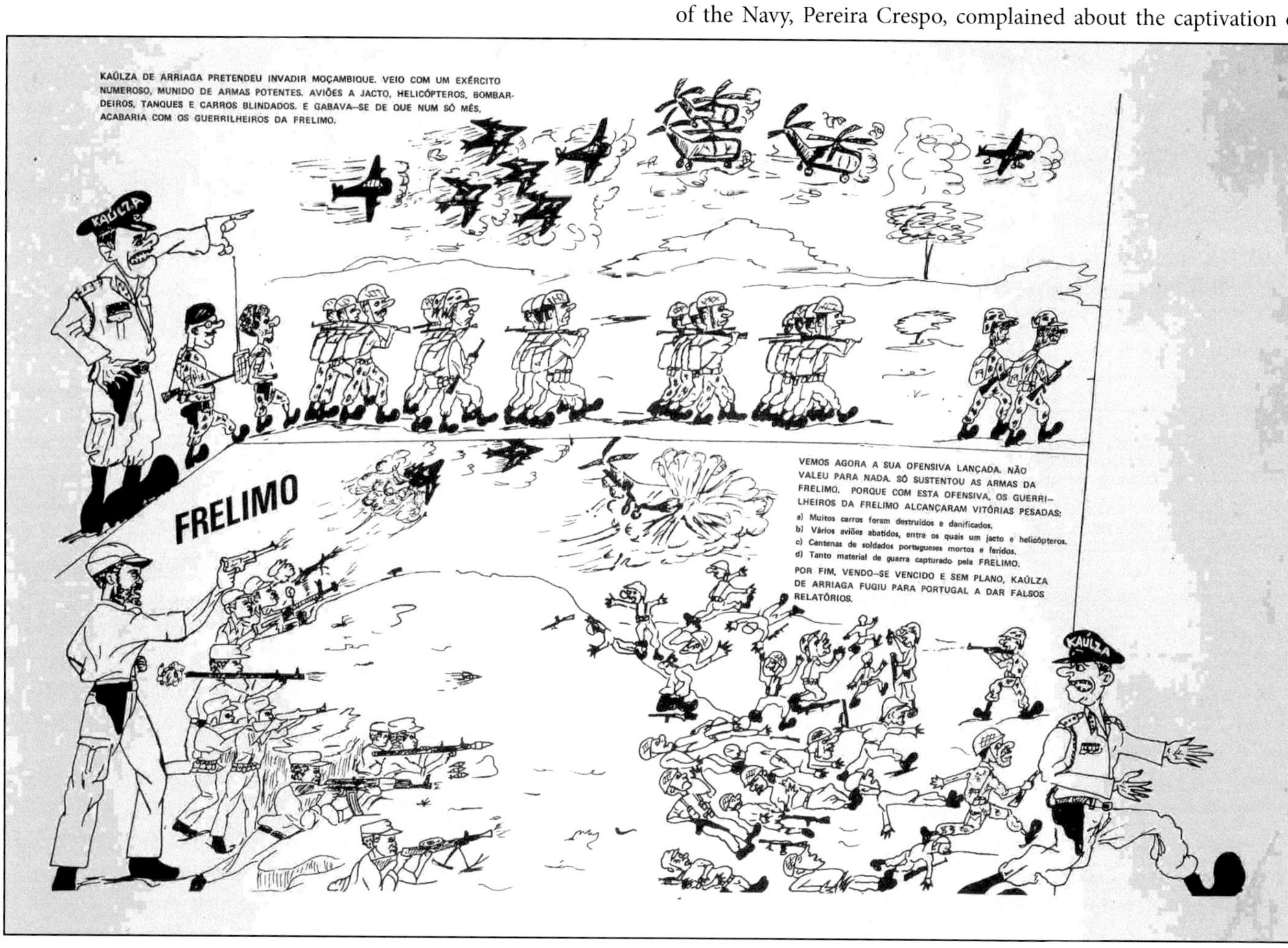

FRELIMO poster ridiculing the action of General Kaúlza de Arriaga during Operation 'Nó Górdio' in 1970. (Miriam Halpern Pereira Collection)

Fiat G-91 5431 Jaguars, landing at AB6, Nova Freixo, Spring 1969. Portugal had two squadrons (Jaguars' and Scorpions) of Fiat G-91 in Mozambique. (Ricardo Barros Collection)

Evacuation of the wounded during the war by an Alouette III helicopter. Portuguese helicopters were very important in this role. (Fernando Farinha Collection)

funds for the works, a problem that was solved during the meeting between Marcello Caetano and the Minister of Finance, Agostinho Dias. Still on Mozambique, Costa Gomes drew attention to the lack of helicopters and Fiat G.91 fighter planes in that territory. The Secretary of State for Aeronautics said that it planned to send 12 more helicopters by the end of the year, but it was not possible to send more Fiat fighters due to the lack of these planes and difficulties in acquisition.[6]

Continuing his exposé, Costa Gomes pointed out that the Mozambican guerrillas (FRELIMO – Front for the Liberation of Mozambique), were already infiltrating the south of Tete and the Zambezi in the central region of Mozambique, and that the Portuguese forces had not been able to contain the guerrillas, having suffered 1,713 casualties in 1973 (237 dead + 1,476 wounded), these numbers being very high. In closing the discussion on Mozambique, Marcello Caetano said that counter-subversion could not be seen only from the military point of view and that all the authorities and services should collaborate in the strategy outlined to control the situation.

After Mozambique, Costa Gomes analysed the situation in Angola, noting that the MPLA (Popular Movement for the Liberation of Angola) led by Agostinho Neto had increased its activity in Cabinda, although without support from the local population and in the military zone in the north of Angola, the situation had evolved in favour of Portuguese interests. However, he drew attention to the deterioration of relations with UNITA (National Union for Total Independence of Angola) and its leader, Jonas Savimbi, who had collaborated with the Portuguese and were now fighting Portuguese troops. On this issue, Marcello Caetano recommended an urgent solution of the matter in order to improve relations with UNITA.

For Costa Gomes, the situation in Angola was much better than in Mozambique, but there was the risk of an attack in Cabinda coming from Zaire with the support of conventional forces, against which Portugal had little chance of defence. To counter such an attack, Portugal needed anti-aircraft defence, combat aviation and anti-tank material, all of which were lacking in the Portuguese arsenal. Once again, Caetano reported the difficulties in obtaining arms

MPLA poster representing Agostinho Neto and the Angolan people with the title: 'A Vitória é Certa' Victory is Sure. (Dalila Cabrita Mateus Collection)

on international markets and that the anti-aircraft missile battery purchased in France, was destined for Guinea. At this point, the Secretary of State for Aeronautics, Tello Polleri, drew attention to the need to continue with the Air Force re-equipment programme, given that recent news foresaw the purchase by Zaire, of Mirage fighters, which could represent a serious threat to the Portuguese forces.[7] At the time, Portugal had no jets in Angola and no defence against an aircraft like the Mirage.

Jonas Savimbi, leader of UNITA and rival of the MPLA and FNLA. After a period of truce, in 1974, he also fought against Portuguese troops. (Reuters)

The Portuguese aviation re-equipment programme also envisaged the acquisition of Mirage fighter jets, the first of which were to be delivered in 1976. Tello Polleri also said that the Air Force had not given up trying to obtain more Fiat fighters in Germany or possibly Italian-made Aermacchi light combat aircraft which were also under consideration, but in either case they were ground attack aircraft that could not be compared to the Mirage.[8] In this regard, the Minister of Foreign Affairs, Rui Patrício, argued that the purchase of French fighter planes was a priority, as they could be decisive for the defence of the country within two years, at a time when Portugal could be even more isolated.

Silva Cunha, Minister of Defence, stressed that the Portuguese forces had great need for armament, that national industry was incapable of responding to the problem, and that it was necessary to buy on the international markets. For the time being, the government had money to meet the most pressing and unpostponable needs, but it seemed to him that additional financing was needed for the purchase of the Mirage. Although he did not say so at the meeting, Silva Cunha knew that the South Africans had recently approved a loan of 150 million rands (6 million contos) to the Portuguese government, which would be channelled in large part, towards the purchase of the French Mirages.[9]

A Mirage 5DM in service with the Zairean Air Force. This country signed in September 1973, a contract with the French for the purchase of 14 Mirage 5M and 3 Mirage DM. (Claudio Toselli Collection)

A Mirage 5 on a demonstration flight. Portugal was initially interested in this version, but ultimately chose the Mirage III for fear of Guinea-Conakry's MiG-17s. (Dassault)

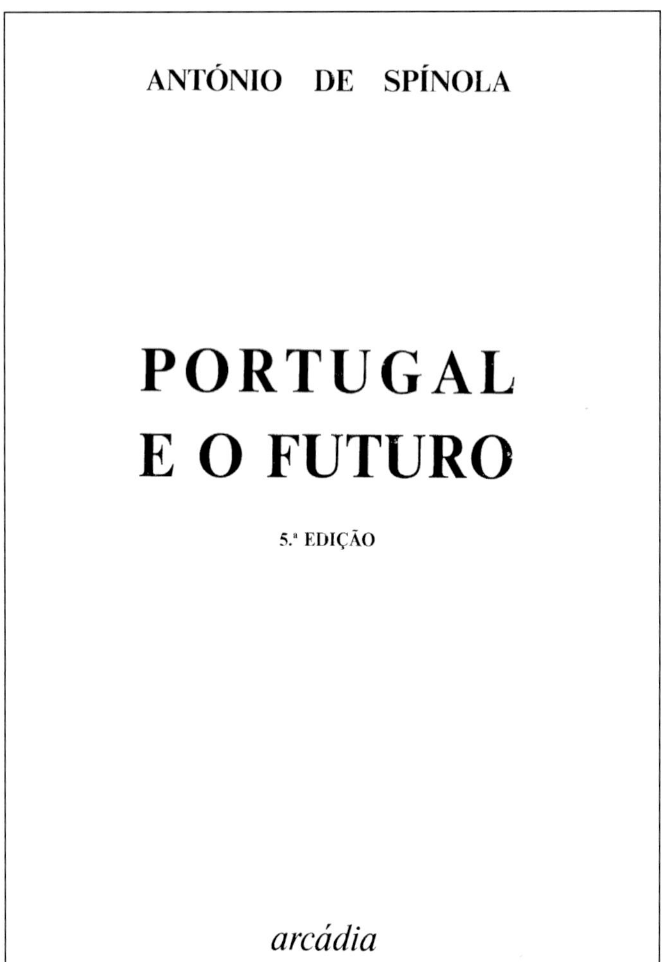

ANTÓNIO DE SPÍNOLA

PORTUGAL
E O FUTURO

5.ª EDIÇÃO

arcádia

Cover of the book *Portugal e o Futuro* (Portugal and the Future) by António Spínola. (José Matos Collection)

However, at this level, Marcello Caetano was concerned about the threats mentioned and that it was urgent to find solutions with the means available as soon as possible, an urgency that was not compatible with the delivery of the Mirages within the foreseen deadlines. For Caetano, it was clear that the Portuguese could not wait two years for the French fighter planes, other solutions had to be found. After these comments, the meeting ended with the promotion of some Navy officers and Caetano said goodbye to those present, without knowing that Costa Gomes had other thoughts regarding the overseas policy. A month earlier, he had authorised the publication of a book that questioned the war effort in Africa.[10]

General Spínola in his Mercedes through the streets of Lisbon. (AEI)

Three days after the meeting of the Supreme Council of National Defence, the head of the executive received a copy of the book *Portugal e o Futuro* (Portugal and the Future), with a dedication from the author, General António de Spínola, who was number two in the military hierarchy, just after Costa Gomes. Spínola had made a name for himself by leading the war in Portuguese Guinea for several years, but he had quickly realised that wars against guerrillas in Africa were a lost cause and that they could only have a political solution and never a military one. This is what he explained in his book, denouncing the government's inability to solve the overseas problem, which had been dragging on for too long.

Due to the Council of Ministers, Marcello Caetano would not read Spínola's book, from the first to the last page, until dawn on the night of 20 February. When closing the book, the then President of the Council would write in his memoirs that he had understood that the military coup d'état, whose march he had sensed for months, was now inevitable.[11]

The book of the revolution

Marcello Caetano's account shows that he had learnt of the book's content on the eve of its publication. However, Otelo Saraiva de Carvalho, one of the leaders of the Armed Forces Movement (MFA – *Movimento das Forças Armadas*) and strategist of the 25th of April coup, reports that on 2nd February, he met Spínola on a street in Lisbon and the latter told him: 'The guys say they have received several letters from officers protesting against the release of my book and they don't want to let it out. Have you ever seen such a thing?' Otelo replies that he hopes it will be published to show that there are general officers with different ideas from the government and asks him what General Francisco Costa Gomes' position is. Spínola replies, 'There's no problem on that side. Chico (Costa Gomes) is with me.' This being the case, Otelo expresses to him the support of the MFA and that the publication of the book is essential to stir the waters.[12] Spínola's conversation with Otelo shows that there was pressure within the regime not to publish the book, although the existence of protests from officials was hard to believe, given that the book's content, as shall be shown later, was kept very secret.

In his memoirs written in exile, Marcello Caetano confessed that he had heard about the general's intention to write a book in late 1972, when Spínola was still governor and commander-in-chief of Guinea. At that time, not satisfied with the Lisbon government's decision to put an end to the contacts he wanted to develop with the PAIGC leader, Amílcar Cabral, the general decided to write a book with his vision of overseas policy.[13]

Spínola had arrived in Guinea in 1968, still during Salazar's time as head of government, and had tried to give a new dynamic to the war, which had been going on in that territory since 1963 and which was increasingly difficult for the Portuguese troops, given the military capacity of the PAIGC and the support it had in neighbouring countries. Spínola tried to reduce the PAIGC's influence in Guinea with a new policy of social promotion among the local population, as well as trying to neutralise the guerrillas militarily by asking for more resources and more men. However, he quickly realised that a military victory was impossible in that situation and that it was necessary to negotiate with the PAIGC, which he tried to do with the help of the President of Senegal (the country which borders Guinea to the north), Léopold Senghor.

In May 1972, he met with this African leader, who was available to broker a peace process for Guinea. The meeting had been authorised by Lisbon in the expectation that Spínola would not make any commitment to the Senegalese leader.[14] The meeting took place on 18 May, in Cap Skirring, Senegal, near the border with Guinea, and Senghor presented him with a peace plan that proposed a transition period in Guinea of at least 10 years, after which the colony would be given independence.[15] Spínola received Senghor's plan with enthusiasm and it seemed to him a reasonable proposal to solve the problem of Guinea and achieve peace with the PAIGC.

When Caetano told him, in response to the plan, that for the global defence of Overseas Territories, it was preferable to leave Guinea through a military defeat with honour than through a negotiated agreement with the terrorists, opening the way to other negotiations (with the other provinces, causing a domino effect), Spínola was shocked and realised that the government's only solution was to continue the war. The military could be blamed by the political regime for a defeat in Guinea, similar to what had happened in India with the fall of Goa, Damão and Diu in 1961.[16] It was at this moment that he thought of writing the book.[17]

Marcello Caetano in exile in Brazil in May 1974, where he wrote his memoirs. (United Press International Photo)

President Senghor arriving at the African and Malagasy Union Conference in Niger in 1968. Senghor tried with Spínola to find a negotiated solution for Guinea which was refused by Marcello Caetano. (Keystone Press)

Contacts in this sense were still made while Spínola was in Guinea and Paradela de Abreu, editor of Arcádia, was the central figure in the publication of the work. The information that Spínola was working on a book came to Paradela de Abreu through Manuel Belchior, the governor's advisor in Guinea. Initially, the editor thought that the general was writing a book about the war in Guinea and went to Bissau to talk to Spínola, but he said little about the theme of the work [18]. Only after negotiating the publication rights,

The Apolo 70 shopping centre in Lisbon. It was in the bookshop of this shopping centre that the first copies of Spínola's book arrived on 22 February 1974. They sold out in a few hours. (Lisbon Municipal Archive)

Spínola giving a speech on the day he took up his duties as Vice-CEMGFA. On the right we can see Costa Gomes (wearing glasses) listening to the speech.(Diário de Notícias)

did Paradela de Abreu have access to the book, in October 1973. He immediately understood that the book was the revolution [19].

Spínola asked him for maximum secrecy regarding the book's content and Paradela de Abreu kept the information to himself, with few people inside the publishing house knowing the true subject of the work. Afraid that the book would be censored or even seized, Abreu spread the printing by several printing companies and in December 1973, the book was ready to be revised by Spínola. After several editorial setbacks, the book went on sale on 22 February 1974. On that day, 2,000 copies were taken to Lisbon's Apollo bookshop, having sold out in a few hours. The book was a resounding success. Nobody understood how it was possible that it was not seized or had even been published. On the same day, the front page of the *República* newspaper carried a headline that was considered bombastic: 'Exclusively military victory is unfeasible – writes General Spínola in his book *Portugal e o Futuro* (Portugal and the Future), which went on sale today' [20]. The newspaper had managed to access the contents of the book and quoted passages from it in abundance with Spínola's main theses about the unfeasibility of war and the urgent need to find a political solution for the Overseas Territories. *República* also said that the book had been rumoured for some time, creating an atmosphere of great expectation and that Spínola was approaching the overseas problem in a way that the Portuguese were not used to seeing. For the former commander of Guinea, no more time could be wasted with postponements; now was the time to find solutions. Finally, the newspaper ended by informing readers that the book would be on sale that day in all bookshops in Lisbon and Porto and the following week in the rest of the country [21].

Another newspaper that publicised the book's release was *Expresso*. The front page featured a photo of Spínola announcing that the book proposed a political restructuring of the country in which a free referendum would legitimise authority. In the pages of the second section, the newspaper explained the general's main theses, predicting that 'due to the subjects covered and the author's courage and experience' the book was sure to become a 'bestseller' in national politics [22].

When he published the book, Spínola was Vice-Chief of Staff of the Armed Forces (Vice-CEMGFA), a post created exclusively for him after he returned from Guinea [23]. The decision to create this post for the former commander of Guinea was not well accepted by the President of the Republic, Admiral Américo Thomaz, who regretted not having been consulted by the President of the Council on the matter. Thomaz was only consulted by the Minister of Defence, Silva Cunha, on the matter and immediately expressed his opposition, but the minister went ahead with the creation of the post. For the head of state, necessity did not impose, or even advise, the creation of the post expressly destined for one person. Besides, Thomaz did not like to see two general officers at the head of the armed forces (the other was Costa Gomes), who could cause difficulties to the policy followed overseas.

The head of state's suspicions became manifest soon after Spínola took office as Vice-CEMGFA, on 17 January 1974. On that day, the then Defence Minister recalls, he learnt that the general had a book ready for publication. Silva Cunha reacted by stating that under the terms of the Armed Forces Officers' Statute, a serving officer could not publish any work without superior authorisation [24]. In the afternoon of that day, Spínola was received by Marcello Caetano, to whom he confirmed that he intended to publish a book of his authorship soon, a work that had the essential purpose of 'making public opinion aware of the acceptance of the overseas theses he defended.' Caetano, following Silva Cunha's proposal, asked the general if he was authorised to publish the book, since the military regulations do not allow him to do so without complying with this formality. Spínola replied that he was not aware of such rules but promised that he would speak to Costa Gomes 'his immediate boss' to obtain authorisation [25].

Given the national and international prestige that the general had achieved during his campaign in Guinea, Marcello did not or could not prohibit the publication. According to his son, Miguel Caetano, the episode of the authorisation of the publication of the book 'is not entirely clear,' the President of the Council would have had an attitude of not conflicting with the Armed Forces, because he could not live without their support and since he understood that the legitimacy of the New State resided in the military [26].

On the other hand, the responsibility for the book's release was officially placed on the CEMGFA, Costa Gomes, who would issue a favourable opinion on 11 February 1974, accompanied by a visa from the Minister of National Defence, Silva Cunha, although the minister confessed that he had never seen the book.

According to Costa Gomes' opinion, the book 'presents, in a very elevated way, the solution that [António Spínola] deems best to solve the greatest problem the nation is facing – the war in Overseas.' Also, according to the document, the general 'logically defends a balanced solution located more or less in the middle of two extreme

The Minister of Defence, Silva Cunha, greeting Spínola on the day he took office as Vice-CEMGFA. Silva Cunha would give a favourable opinion on the book, however, without reading it.(Diário de Notícias)

solutions that have been widely debated: that of independence, pure, simple and immediate independence of all the Overseas Territories, supported by the communists and socialists, and that of the integration in a homogenous whole of all those parts, as advocated by the right-wing extremists.'

Costa Gomes concluded: 'We do not need to develop a great deal of argumentation to conclude that these solutions should be set aside, the first because it is harmful to national interests and the second because it is unfeasible.' In this sense, he considered that the book would be in a position to be published [27]. The way Costa Gomes' opinion was written leaves no doubt that, like Spínola, he also believed that the time had come for the government to find a solution for the war [28].

Regarding this opinion, the President of the Republic wrote, also in his memoirs, that, as it was a much more political and economic book than military, the CEMGFA should not have been asked for an opinion, nor should the authorisation for publication be based upon it. In short, Thomaz considered the opinion a mistake and that neither Caetano nor Silva Cunha were up to the positions they held in authorising the book [29].

In turn, showing the discomfort of the situation, Silva Cunha stressed in his opinion of a few lines, that he did not know the text and that the agreement he gave was based only on the opinion expressed by Costa Gomes. Silva Cunha expressed this concern to Marcello Caetano, finding it strange that the general avoided showing him the book, but Caetano considered that the withdrawal of the work was preferable to the scandal of the 'forbidden book,' which would erupt inside and outside the country, with the government being accused of hiding the authoritative and patriotic opinion of a prestigious military chief. Moreover, Costa Gomes had given his assent and the CEMGFA was the government's principal military adviser. Silva Cunha reluctantly accepted Caetano's decision and a few days later, received an autographed copy of the book confirming his worst fears [30].

However, this version of events was later contradicted by Costa Gomes. According to the CEMGFA, it was precisely the Minister of Defence who handed him the photocopies received from the hands of the Director General of Security (DGS – the name given to the regime's political police, which at the time of the previous head of government, Oliveira Salazar, was called PIDE – *Polícia Internacional e de Defesa do Estado),* Major Silva Pais, with whom Silva Cunha met daily. For Costa Gomes, only those who did not know the working method of the DGS could imagine that the book, once printed, would not be of Silva Cunha's immediate knowledge. At the very least, Silva Pais would have informed the Minister of the issue dealt with in the book. Costa Gomes claims that what happened was 'that he [Silva Cunha] did not want to take responsibility for the publication of the book,' referring this responsibility to the Chief of Staff [31]. However, there is no evidence that the full content of the book was known at the DGS and that it had come to Silva Cunha's knowledge.[32] As previously mentioned, Paradela de Abreu was always very careful to keep the contents of the book secret and never mentions that the book in any way, came to the knowledge of the political police. At this level, there is the testimony of Augusto de Sá Viana Rebelo, deputy in the National Assembly and president of the Corporation of Industry, who mentions in his memoirs having spoken with Silva Cunha (of whom he had been a course mate) and heard the minister say that he had not read the book and that the responsibility of giving an opinion rested with Costa Gomes.[33] This testimony seems to confirm that the contents of the book did not really come to Silva Cunha's knowledge before its publication.

Since late 1970, Marcello Caetano knew Spínola's political thought regarding the Overseas Territories and the war problem. At that time, Spínola was governor and commander-in-chief of the Guinea Armed Forces, and at Marcello's request, he prepared a document entitled 'Some ideas on the political structuring of the nation,' as a contribution to the 1971 constitutional revision. This document would, in fact, be at the origin of *Portugal e o Futuro*. There, Spínola clearly defended greater autonomy for the colonies and a federative solution between Portugal and the Overseas Territories. In the document, the general warned that the most serious problem facing Portugal was the problem of the Overseas Territories and that only a federal solution would safeguard national unity and prevent the future loss of the African territories.[34] Spínola later tried to incorporate some of his ideas into the statute of Guinea, which was revised in 1972, but he did not succeed.[35] Marcello Caetano also knew what Spínola thought about the war, since in May 1971, in a meeting of the Higher Council of National Defence (CSDN), he had categorically stated that the regime should lose any vague desire to win the war militarily, 'which could only be won in the field of weapons in the face of an unpredictable turn in the present world situation,' a situation that was not in sight in the horizon.[36]

It is likely that before reading *Portugal e o Futuro*, Marcello was convinced that the work fundamentally defended the federative solution to the overseas question. Both had exchanged opinions on the subject over time with Spínola advocating a federative solution and negotiations with the nationalist movements, while Caetano refused any negotiations with the guerrillas who, in his opinion, were interested in expelling the whites from Africa [37]. Still in this context, he thought that Spínola, who had been invested in new functions a little over a month before (on 17 January 1974) as Vice-CEMGFA, in a position of trust of the government, would maintain some loyalty towards those who had appointed him.

Marcello Caetano working in the morning at home with his personal assistant. (Lisbon Photography Archive/Portuguese Centre of Photography)

In this sense, when he realised that, in addition to the federalist thesis, the general insisted in the book that a solution by force of arms was unfeasible, in a position directly against the government that defended the sustainability of war, he immediately summoned the two generals (Costa Gomes and Spínola) for a not very pleasant conversation on the following day, 22 February – a Friday, at 11:00 a.m. in his house (mornings were usually spent working at home).

A day earlier, on 21 February, Spínola had handed a copy to the Head of State and told Américo Thomaz that the work was only intended as a personal contribution to the resolution of the problems affecting the country, including the war in Africa. In the dedication that accompanied the book, Spínola justified himself by saying that he was convinced that he was 'rendering the country a service at a serious time in which it is not licit to refuse to contribute to the common effort of pursuing the greatness of Portugal.'[38] This justification did not please the President of the Republic, for whom the Portuguese overseas problem could only have one of two solutions: the one that had been in course for more than a decade, that is, the search for military victory, through the fight that had been waged against terrorism and other forms of terrorism for 13 years, in defence of the sacred integrity of the homeland, or the pure and simple handing over of the Portuguese territories of Angola, Guinea and Mozambique, to the terrorist movements that were attacking them.

Thomaz says that Spínola still replied that between the two extremes, there were certainly several possible solutions, including his own, which he admitted might not be the best. Thomaz replied that there was no point in having illusions, since there were only the two solutions he mentioned.[39]

In *Portugal e o Futuro*, Spínola states that the core of the main national problem – the situation of the African colonies – is to 'know whether a military solution is feasible in war (...); and, failing that, what are the consequences of indefinitely sustaining a situation revealed to be unviable and what are the limits of capacity for it.'

For Spínola, one can thus reach the conclusion that, in any war of this type [between a colony and movements for the self-

Spínola and Thomaz at a ceremony at the Military College, after the general had returned from Guinea. The two men obviously did not share the same vision on the Overseas problem. (Revista do Povo collection)

determination of peoples], exclusively military victory is unviable. 'The Armed Forces only have the task, therefore, of creating and preserving for the necessary period – naturally not a very long one – the security conditions that will permit political and social solutions, the only ones capable of putting an end to the conflict (...) To pretend to win a subversive war by means of a military solution is to accept defeat beforehand, unless one has unlimited capacity to prolong the war indefinitely, turning it into an institution. Is that the case for us?'[40]

António Spínola continued, however, to believe in maintaining the Portuguese presence overseas as a condition for the survival of Portugal as a free and independent nation. 'Without the African territories, the country will be reduced to an insignificant corner of a growing Europe (...). We shall remain in Africa. Yes! But not by force of arms (...) but by a clear vision of the problems within the framework of a Portuguese solution.'[41]

The general felt that the country should not be intimidated by positions of irreducibility, which forced a direct choice between two impossibilities when there could be other, more Portuguese, solutions. 'Reducing the overseas question to extreme positions and presenting the country with the dilemma of perpetuating the war or betraying the past, is an attitude that does not lead to the future,' argued Spínola.[42] The solution implied, according to the author, the recognition of the right of peoples to self-determination, a principle that points to a progressive autonomy, in a climate of growing expression of African institutions. In this sense, he advocated recourse to popular consultation, a process which would only work if widely publicised.[43]

As already noted, on February 22, the two generals then appeared at Marcello Caetano's house in uniform for a conversation 'of the most serious and unpleasant' ones of his life, although Marcello declined to reproduce its exact terms. For the President of the Council, the book could only influence the mood of the Armed Forces regarding the maintenance of the war and weigh on public opinion regarding the directions of domestic policy, besides reducing the Portuguese government's already narrow margin for manoeuvre in the international context.

Feeling unauthorised, he understood that it was manifestly impossible for him to continue governing with officers who were unsubmissive and disagreed with the government's policy. However, he felt that at that moment, he should not be the one to ask for resignation, as it was not him who had published what he considered to be a 'manifesto.' He felt that everyone should assume their responsibilities. For Caetano, the 'manifesto' reflected the intention of a coup d'état, and it was necessary not to let the situation deteriorate. According to Marcello, the government had been left in a delicate situation since the divorce between it and the highest representatives of the military hierarchy, was open. In this sense, he argued that the generals should reclaim power from the Head of State.

Caetano reported that the proposal made to the generals was listened to in silence. 'Spínola reaffirmed that he was a disciplined military man who did not take part in conspiracies or give coups d'état.' Costa Gomes advised Marcello Caetano to be patient, as there would be no remedy but to continue to make the sacrifice of being in government, but he understood that the analysis made by Spínola in the book, corresponded to reality, although this did not inhibit the government from continuing to govern. However, Caetano insisted that he was not in a position to continue with authority in the policy he had maintained up to that point and that the two generals should really talk to the President of the Republic.[44]

Still in the context of the conversation, Spínola justified the book in the light of the country's worsening situation and that the opinions expressed there were contained in several opinions and proposals delivered to Marcello over time, with no practical consequences. He therefore 'understood that the time had come to make public opinion aware in order to create the human conditions that would enable the government to solve the national crisis in the realistic light of possible solutions, and he saw no reason why he – Marcello Caetano – should not continue at the head of the government,' thus ruling out any possibility of talks with Américo Thomaz. Costa Gomes agreed with this position and refused any possibility of taking power.[45] In the opinion of the two generals, Caetano should continue to govern.

Later, Spínola would also say that it was 'urgent to counterbalance the pressures of the ultra-right current [which was influential in the President of the Republic] – advocating a monolithic solution – with the weight of the majority will of the nation, which needed to be clarified in order to open up to solutions in line with the current realities.' In his opinion, it was necessary for the Portuguese people, in addition to the direct choice between two impossibilities, to be aware of alternatives. The question was only presented as the institutionalisation of war, military defeat, or betrayal of the past, an attitude that did not lead to a future which the Portuguese legitimately aspired.[46]

The book had a great impact on public opinion, selling out quickly in bookshops. Pedro Feytor Pinto, who was the director of the Information Services of the Secretariat of State for Information and Tourism and in this post, responsible for press relations, recounts that he bought the book in a Lisbon bookshop for 100 escudos, after having shortly met the ambassador, Calvet Magalhães in the street, who asked him how much it had cost. On hearing the price of the book, the ambassador exclaimed: 'The future of Portugal for 100 escudos is cheap! I'll buy it right away!'[47] Feytor Pinto admits that in certain aspects the book coincided with Caetano's thinking, but that it could create a confrontational situation with the President of the Council.[48]

Other personalities with whom Spínola had relations, also received the book. This was the case of Francisco Sá Carneiro, former member of parliament from the Liberal Wing, who had broken with Marcello Caetano. Sá Carneiro thought the book 'truly remarkable' and felt that the country had Spínola to thank for a work that opened up 'new perspectives in a closed horizon full of despondency.' He also calculated the book's impact would not easily disappear, certainly having consequences in the short term.[49]

Spínola autographing the book to readers months later. There is no doubt that the book shook the regime.(Diário de Notícias)

Francisco Sá Carneiro, a former member of the liberal wing of parliament, broke with the regime when he realised that the country was at a dead end. After the Carnation Revolution he would become one of the most important politicians in Portugal, becoming Prime Minister in the late 1970s. (José Matos Collection)

Adriano Moreira, who had been Minister of Overseas under Salazar, also read the book and wrote a letter to Spínola on 15 April, confessing that he was very surprised by the attempt to confuse Spínola's proposal with Marcello Caetano's former thinking on federalism, which was, in his opinion, an attempt to 'establish the imperial model of the British community.' Moreira did not commit himself to Spínola's proposals but said that 'I will always be pleased to analyse with Your Excellency the implications of the proposals you put forward in your important work.'[50]

However, of the correspondence exchanged with various personalities regarding the book, the most interesting is with António Ramalho Eanes, who after the April Revolution would become Portugal's first democratically elected President of the Republic.[51] Eanes was a major at the time and had been with Spínola in Guinea when the general was commander and governor of the colony and after having read the book, he sent him a letter and a telegram of congratulations. As he wrote on 11 April, already after Spínola's exoneration from the post of Vice-CEMGFA, Eanes severely criticised the ceremony of vassalage of the generals to the political power, in which Spínola refused to participate, saying that it was nothing but a 'low-style farce, represented by the gentlemen generals, before the president of the Council.' For him, the true generals were those 'that we met in the bush, in the sting, in the intelligent and opportune decision, conscious and above all responsible, generals that have fought for this alienated Army to gain consciousness again of its historical and national dimension!'

In the same context, Eanes considered that the true Army was 'the one which is still able to fight for the nation and for its real interests – the one which no longer accepts farces, just as it no longer tolerates its actor-generals. It accepts as symbol and reality Spínola and others who may also be capable of being Spínolas.' On the book itself, Ramalho Eanes stated that 'personally I may, after sufficient study, opt for regionalisation or Federation, as the most convenient political solution for the interests of the nation. But I do not need study to state that I unconditionally share all the other sectoral or global perspectives, defined with meridian clarity by my general. I would add that today the admiration, friendship, and dedication that my general deserves from me is even greater.'[52] In his reply, on 19 April, Spínola thanked him for his words and told him that he had written the book so that 'the nation would awake from the lethargic sleep into which a great mass of the Portuguese has fallen' and also considered that 'the homeland is seriously ill' and that the political elites were leading the country to ruin.[53]

The book was also commented on in diplomatic circles. At the American embassy in Lisbon, ambassador Stuart Nash Scott analysed the book at length for the State Department and commented that Spínola's proposals left open the possibility of complete independence for the African territories, a fact that struck Portugal like a bolt from the sky. Scott acknowledges that Spínola's military prestige giave him a legitimacy of his own to put forward such bold proposals and that the general had political ambitions, for the book is a 'self-appointment to national leadership.'[54]

The French embassy in Lisbon, meanwhile, referred to the book's release as a major political event as it questioned the official truths with unprecedented clarity. Since 4 March, ambassador Bernard Durand had been reporting almost daily, to the French government on the political crisis in Portugal, sparked by the release of *Portugal e o Futuro*. On 1 March, the diplomat wrote six pages in which he gave his opinion on the book and summarised its contents. For Durand, federalism, democratisation, liberalisation were the key words in the authorised work, uncut by censorship (which had been in force in the country for decades) and written by someone close to the regime. The book was presented to Portuguese public opinion, more as a set of critical reflections than a programme. Moreover, its value lay essentially, in the questioning of current political norms and methods, since solutions were often superficial, while the means to implement them were practically avoided. Perhaps this was why the liberal and left-wing press was so interested in the book, in which they found a reflection of their views but did not say much about that of the establishment of a federation.

The French ambassador also noted that the circles of the extreme right were silent, that their reaction was difficult to predict and they should not ignore the prestige that General Spínola had acquired in the Army, particularly during his time in Guinea. Nor should the growing dissatisfaction of public opinion be ignored, disorientated by the sluggishness of government action, disarmed by the ravages of inflation and the attacks on their already mediocre standard of living and worried by the prospect of a dead-end war.[55]

In a later telegram, the diplomat revealed he had a conversation with Spínola on 9 March and began by noting that the general had a continuous military career but had not been noticed until his appointment as commander-in-chief of Guinea-Bissau and now, with his book. He recounted that Spínola told him that the work was the fruit of reflections that he decided to share with the Portuguese people, as well as suggesting solutions such as the federation of equal states, referring also to contacts he had with Senghor. However, 'my interlocutor seemed disconcerted by the reaction of Caetano,' whom he considered close to his ideas, and justified that the book had been submitted to the military hierarchy and the head of the government.

Despite the reaction of the President of the Council, the general confessed that he was not prepared to take the consequences of the situation and resign from his functions. Spínola also told the French

Captain António Ramalho Eanes in Mozambique at the end of 1963, in the house of a local leader. Eanes had a discreet participation in the Armed Forces Movement to overthrow the regime, but after the revolution, he became a military man in the limelight, reaching the Presidency of the Republic. (Museum of the Presidency of the Republic)

diplomat that the National Assembly, which had just approved on 5 March a motion accepting the regime's overseas policy, had zero representation. According to the general, Caetano was more concerned with the reactions the book provoked abroad than with the ideas it contained.

Finally, Durand pointed out that 'after 45 years in which everything written was subject to censorship, the publication of a book condemning to failure the policy pursued by the government in the Overseas Territories, predicting self-determination, a referendum (...)' could only give the impression to the outside world that Portugal was about to evolve, or at least the internal front was shaken due to the publication of such a polemical book.[56]

It was in Guinea that Spínola achieved stardom, gaining national and international projection. Here he is shown in a bush operation with officers of his confidence during a report for the French magazine *Paris-Match*. (Genevieve Chauvel/Sygma/Getty)

The captains conspire

After the conversation with the two generals, Marcello went on a rest for a few days (Carnival holiday) in Buçaco, in the centre of the country. At that time, while the head of government was out of the capital, the leadership of the captains' movement, called the Executive Coordinating Commission (CCE – *Comissão Coordenadora Executiva*), met in Lisbon on 25 February, at Otelo Saraiva de Carvalho's home.

According to Otelo, delegates from the main Army units were present: delegates from the paratroops – Silva Pinto, Bação de Lemos and Avelar de Sousa; the practical school captains, Rui Rodrigues from the Infantry Practical School (EPI); Salgueiro Maia from the Cavalry Practical School (EPC) and Heitor Alves from the Artillery Practical School (EPA) and Manuel Trigo from the Special Operations Training Centre (CIOE). Air Force captains Balacó and Seabra were also present. The meeting was also attended by Major Melo Antunes and a representative of the Mozambique Military Region, Captain Ruivo de Oliveira.

The drafting commission presented three texts that sought to politically define the movement and it was decided that the representatives of the units should listen to each unit, sending Vasco Lourenço the suggestions in a registered letter by 3 March. Those present were to collect the fundamental ideas from the three documents and transmit the essentials to the officers in service in the units, seeking to hear criticism and opinions. The distributed copies would not leave the room for security reasons. They also decided to hold an enlarged meeting (which they called a mini-plenary) with a minimum of one delegate per unit, who would sign the document immediately after reading it, mentioning, for control purposes, how many he represented and how many he linked to the content of the manifesto.

'We were moved by haste,' remembers Otelo, who also shows that he was apprehensive with the implications of Spínola's book in the national and international public opinion and especially with what he called the 'inversion of values.' In other words:

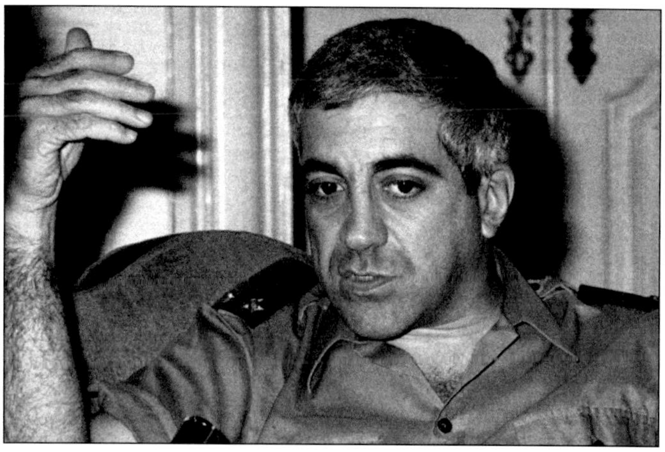

Otelo Saraiva de Carvalho was one of the main leaders of the Armed Forces Movement (MFA) and responsible for the operations plan that overthrew the regime on 25 April. After the revolution, Otelo took on important functions as military commander of Lisbon. (Revista do Povo collection)

> No one would later stop considering Spínola to have been the real brain and mentor of the movement, and his work (...) the lighthouse that had enlightened the young officers and guided them to a good port, when what actually happened was precisely the opposite: the movement walked safely and firmly, without needing and without resorting to the general's advice in any definition of its ideology. It was Spínola, in fact, who needed the strength and impulse of the movement in order to achieve, in the near future, what he longed for.[57]

However, despite Otelo's concerns, it was obvious that Spínola's book created an additional motivation for MFA officers to feel that the political situation had to change radically.

The first government of Marcello Caetano in 1968. Next to Marcello is Viana Rebelo (in uniform), who took over as Minister of National Defence. Viana Rebelo was the one who provided the face for the measures taken in 1973 to solve the problem of the lack of officers in the Army, which provoked discontent among the career officers. (Diário de Notícias)

The mini-plenary was scheduled for 5 March, considering that the Air Force Commission and the drafting committee would have enough time to draft their own document and the Army's final document respectively. Air Force and Navy representations would also attend the 5 March meeting.

Once it was concretely established how strong the movement really was – what the policy was and how many (number of signatures) adherents – there were two hypotheses to consider: either they would present their demands to the government or they would present them to a leader, who would meet their objectives and agree to lead the movement.

Otelo noted the lack of confidence of some of those present, in the strength of the movement, needing someone 'who really knew about these political things.' At this meeting, Captain Ruivo de Oliveira declared his total and absolute solidarity of those serving in Mozambique with those in the metropolis. It was decided that the movement would react to any reprisal against its elements. As a precautionary measure, each member of the Executive Coordinating Committee chose a substitute to fill their vacancy in the event of arrests. At this stage, they decided to request a meeting between the leadership and representatives of the officers from the Complementary Staff, in order to clarify the movement's objectives and try to bring together efforts.

The organisation of the movement would be extended with the creation of regional commissions (grouping members serving in nearby units, with the members of these commissions having the mission of, at least one, going to the meetings of the CCE in Lisbon). These would be represented in the meetings of the coordinating commission in order to be in touch with the issues discussed there, functioning even in the case of the total elimination of the CCE due to the repression by power [58].

Close to what was happening in the movement, António Spínola was informed by a man he trusted, Captain António Ramos, of what was happening, even before he took up his post as Vice-CEMGFA on 17 January. A few days after assuming his new duties, he received in his office, at the Cova da Moura Palace, elements of the captains' movement. A delegation of four militia captains, Alberto Ferreira, Andrade Moura, Pais de Faria and Armando Ramos, handed him a document signed by 200 militia officers. Spínola suggested to them 'that they should meet with the commission representing the Academy captains in order to study together a proposal that would satisfy both parties, which should be handed to him to constitute a working basis.'[59] Captain António Ramos was also present at this meeting. In the document handed to Spínola, it could be read that they had come to appeal to Spínola's 'legendary spirit of justice and combatant solidarity' to intercede with the government 'in favour of a fair solution' for the great problem that also afflicted militia officers.[60]

Unrest in the military

The problem of seniority went back to the decrees (353/73, 23 July 1973) and (409/73, 20 August 1973), published in the summer of 1973. The government's goal was to combat the shortage of career officers by facilitating access to the Permanent Staff (QP – *Quadro Permanente*) by militia officers. The issue had been analysed in a meeting of the Higher Military Council (CSM – *Conselho Superior Militar*) on 24 March, which was attended by the Minister of National Defence, Viana Rebelo, the CEMGFA, Costa Gomes and the heads of the three branches. The purpose of the CSM meeting was to list measures to improve the situation of the QP officers. The low affluence of candidates to the Military Academy, the abandonment of service by senior officers and the general fatigue due to the mobilisation in successive commissions in the war in Africa, were factors that were shaking the Army and measures had to be taken. The recourse to militia officers, who through short courses would pass to the permanent staff, without loss of seniority, appeared as the quickest measure to solve the problem, although it was recognised that the lack of culture and technical preparation, besides the professional difference in relation to the officers coming from the Military Academy were inconveniences to be considered.[61]

However, this was the path followed by the Minister of Defence, Viana Rebelo and the two diplomas framing the situation were approved in meetings of the Council of Ministers without much opposition, except for that of the Minister of the Navy, Vice-Admiral Pereira Crespo [62].

When it came into force, officers from the militia would overtake those from the cadets in the Permanent Staff in their careers, a situation they considered to be an injustice. The second decree tried to remedy this, but only in the case of senior officers. Captains and non-captains still felt disadvantaged. This feeling was clearly expressed in Bissau on 28 August 1973, when 47 captains signed a letter addressed to the President of the Republic, the President of the Council, the Ministers of Defence and Education and the Secretary of State for the Army:

> The captains of the QP, in service in the province of Guinea, having become aware of the content of Decree-Law 353/73 and its subsequent amendment, have come to make known their deep regret and amazement at finding that the new wording of articles

Manuel Pereira Crespo, Minister of the Navy arrives in Bissau in January 1971 for an official visit. Pereira Crespo was a friend of Spínola and was the only minister who expressed reservations regarding the measures advocated by Viana Rebelo. (Álvaro B. Geraldo Collection)

3 and 6 of the same Decree-Law in almost no way attenuates the recognised deficiencies of which its first form suffered.

The officers, former cadets from Military Academy, said that they were 'wounded in their prestige, their dignity, their professional pride and intellectual eclecticism on learning that the Military Academy course that they had attended for four years could be replaced by a two-semester intensive course.' For these men, this was a 'flagrant inversion of values.' As regards the revocation of articles 3 and 6, they considered that 'the alterations introduced only rectified situations that affected senior officers and did not consider the position of the QP, who had been and still were, the ones who had borne the greatest burden of the hardness of the African campaigns and the training of troops in the metropolis.'[63]

On 14 September 1973, a telegram from the Angolan governor Santos e Castro, arrived in Luanda to the Minister of Overseas Territories, Silva Cunha, in which the governor reported a conversation he had with the commander-in-chief of the Angolan Armed Forces, General Luz Cunha. In this, the latter expressed 'his great concern' about what he called a 'deep schism created between QP officers and complementary officers as a result of the conditions for admitting militiamen to the Military Academy and their integration into the QP military career.' The governor warned of the existence of political exploitation from outside military circles and of the circulation of pamphlets that had arrived from Lisbon.

Two weeks later, Santos Castro sent a new telegram stating that the situation of contestation against the government's diplomas had worsened and that the situation in Mozambique was identical.[64] The agitation in military circles was also reported by the DGS delegation in Luanda in two secret reports dated 15 and 26 October.[65] It is worth noting that Costa Gomes and Viana Rebelo were aware of the problem and that Rebelo passed through Luanda on 27 September, speaking at the time with Luz Cunha. Probably as a result of this conversation, the minister issued an order on 18 October to the Directorate of Personnel of the Army Ministry, so that the impact of the decrees on the officers' careers would be carefully studied for later analysis at ministerial level.[66]

Still in October, during a lunch at the EPA – *Escola Prática de Artilharia* (Artillery Practical School), in Vendas Novas, the Secretary of State for the Army, Brigadier José Alberty Correia,

Viana Rebelo at a NATO meeting in 1971. In late 1973, Caetano replaced him in the Portuguese government. Silva Cunha became the new Minister of Defence. (NATO Collection)

Official family portrait of the Governor-General of Mozambique, Baltazar Rebelo de Sousa in 1968. In 1973, Marcello Caetano called him into the government to take charge of the Ministry of Overseas Territories. (Museum of the Presidency)

criticised the decrees, despite defending them with the conviction that their implementation would allow the problem of the lack of officers in the Army, which was extremely worrying, to be solved.[67]

Aware of the climate of contestation and dissatisfaction, Marcello Caetano promoted a ministerial reshuffle on 7 November, replacing Viana Rebelo and Alberty Correia with Silva Cunha in Defence and Andrade e Silva in the Army.[68] The Ministry of Overseas Territories was taken over by Baltazar Rebelo de Sousa, who had been governor of Mozambique, and Viana de Lemos became Under-Secretary of State for the Army. The reshuffle took place shortly after the legislative elections for the National Assembly, which took place on 28 October. 150 deputies were elected, all from the regime's party, since the opposition did not run as they felt the elections were not free.

The new ministerial team in defence decided to revoke the controversial decree-laws in an attempt to demobilise the captains' movement by eliminating the reasons for the protest. In addition, they created the conditions for the immediate promotion of 200 officers to the ranks of colonel, lieutenant-colonel and major. At the end of 1973, the government also approved new salary scales that allowed for substantial increases in the salaries of the armed forces.[69] At the time, Otelo Saraiva de Carvalho feared the demobilisation of the movement, but this did not happen [70].

Spínola and Silva Cunha (left in glasses and hat) in Guinea in 1970. Relations between the two were always good, but in the final phase of the regime Spínola no longer told him everything he knew. (Álvaro B. Geraldo Collection)

developing a personal action with the high commands and other general officers in evidence.

The Vice-CEMGFA intended to integrate the movement of captains in a 'global strategy' that would enable a 'dignified' solution to the overseas problem. He added that this would pave the way for the institutionalisation of a democratic state in line with the countries of free Europe.[74]

Despite officially receiving the elements of the movement, Spínola informed Marcello (on 7 March) that he spoke to them in 'the clear language of discipline,' considering that 'without discipline there is no Army.'[75] The then Minister of Defence would only respond to Spínola a few years after the events.

Silva Cunha argues that Spínola betrayed the trust of those who had appointed him to the high office he held and which he had accepted voluntarily, violating the most elementary duties of military ethics and simple common morality, which required him to loyally warn his superiors of what was happening and to use his prestige and authority to restore discipline. Instead, he resolved to act against defence policy and began to conspire against the government which had appointed him.[76] Silva Cunha's complaint was justified, since Spínola was aware of the captains' movements and was trying to take advantage of their dissatisfaction.

In a war of words and quoting Spínola himself when he revealed that 'the Minister of Defence and General Costa Gomes, the former through his own sources of information, were aware of the movement's activity,'[77] Silva Cunha replied that it was significant that the general stressed that his knowledge was 'through his own sources of information' and not through him. Silva Cunha explains that such sources gave him very little information, as they had enormous difficulties in keeping up with what was happening in military circles. In spite of this, whenever he received any information, he kept asking for the attention of Generals Spínola and Costa Gomes, who systematically said that there was no reason for concern as they were in a position to guarantee the normality of the situation. 'I don't remember General Spínola ever talking to me about the danger of an armed insurrection when it came to the captains' movement,' Silva Cunha confesses: '(...) I do remember General Spínola insisting several times that I should replace the Director General of Security, Major Silva Pais, suggesting the name of several officers who were invariably trusted by him.' [78] In other words, it seems that Spínola was more concerned with placing a man he trusted at the head of the political police, than informing Silva Cunha of what was happening in the captains' movement.

Still in January 1974, Otelo and Vasco Lourenço were received by Spínola, to whom they reported the situation in Mozambique, namely what had happened in the city of Beira, where the white population had protested against the Portuguese troops. As to be discussed later, the protests had been provoked by the death of a farmer's wife in Manica, an attack carried out by the Mozambican guerrillas of FRELIMO (Front for the Liberation of Mozambique), which angered the white settlers. The protests were violent and surprised the Portuguese troops. Some of the more excited people even stoned the building where the army officers' mess was located in Beira and fired a few pistol shots.[71] In Lisbon, the Government realised the gravity of the situation and sent Costa Gomes to Mozambique to find out what was happening. However, the captains' movement felt that those protests were an offence to the soldiers fighting in the colony and reacted indignantly, demanding reparation for the affront, through a circular that was distributed in several barracks in Portugal [72].

The content of the circular led Spínola to call Otelo and Vasco Lourenço to his office to tell them that the document had an impact in the Army's higher ranks, since the minister and the under-secretary of State had complained to him. Spínola, however, advised the rulers not to retaliate against the captains, as they did not even know who the leaders of the movement were. This was not exactly true, as Spínola knew the military that led the movement and even received them in his office.[73]

Spínola later admitted that:

> In view of the government's incapacity to solve the extremely serious political and military crisis (...), the incipient movement of the captains was irreversible, since it was based on undoubtedly valid reasons, and it should therefore be oriented towards transforming it into a useful force with the military chiefs in charge, forcing them to take a stand. In the same vein, he was

Caetano resigns

Américo Thomaz in his office at the Belém Palace, where he usually received Marcello Caetano. (Museum of the Presidency)

On 26 February 1974, Caetano returned from his holidays in Buçaco and in his correspondence he had a letter from Vítor Manuel de Aguiar e Silva, a university professor and deputy to the National Assembly, who wrote a premonitory missive from Coimbra. The deputy, who had just read Spínola's book, said he had no doubts about the profound and unpredictable consequences it would have on national political life.[79] Aguiar e Silva predicted that the National Assembly would be the place where political life would be most agitated – although without the 'liberal wing' – and considered that the political situation had deteriorated in recent months. He recalled that in the last electoral campaign, he defended a political development that would imply a liberalisation within the regime and not against the regime and that 'the crises such as those that have been experienced for around 13 years, by their very dragging, become elements that generate an ideological and political blockage.' In Aguiar e Silva's view, the crisis would end up leading the country's future to 'two pseudo-solutions: military dictatorship and revolutionary violence.'

However, Marcello reacted and called a restricted Council of Ministers to analyse the publication of the book. It was not possible to determine the date on which it took place (probably 27 February), nor the ministers who were present, but it is known that Vice-Admiral Pereira Crespo, the Minister of the Navy, was one of those who attended the meeting. According to Pereira Crespo's account, Marcello Caetano's bitterness was visible, as he felt abandoned by the Army. The younger officers were conspiring and the top military chiefs seemed to want to follow other directions, therefore, when the meeting ended, Pereira Crespo had no doubt that the head of the government was going to ask the President of the Republic for his resignation.[80] That day, Caetano also met with Pedro Feytor Pinto who was responsible for media relations and insisted that he considered the book a real coup d'état, although he did not disagree with the ideas defended in the book. However, he could not allow a general with Spínola's responsibilities, to attack the government in that way. At the end of the conversation, he revealed that he was going to ask the President of the Republic for his resignation.[81]

Marcello Caetano met Thomaz on the morning of 28 February, in an audience, which lasted an hour and a half. The Admiral, then 80 years old, received Caetano in his office and showed his concerns about the 'inconvenient' diffusion of the book, but went further – what interested him were its main repercussions and its dangerous consequences, given the climate it had created and aggravated.[82] The President regretted 'the ambition and the little sense of the author,' referring to 'the weaknesses with which the case had been approached' and 'had the impression' that the ministers of Defence and of the Interior, were not properly alerted to the mounting dangers. For Thomaz, the book constituted a 'bad and dangerous flag,' not because of its real value, but because it was an opportunity offered to those who, in his view, attacked the government and the regime of the country.

Marcello, on the other hand, related this hearing, saying that he told Thomaz of the interview he had with the two generals and the advice he had given them (to reclaim power from the Presidency), which they did not do. Caetano said that the publication of the book, coming from where it did, was serious in itself, but was made even more serious by the occasion on which it occurred, giving a doctrine and lending a flag to the so-called 'movement of the captains' with which the general had repeatedly stated he did not identify. Marcello also took the opportunity to tell the President of the Republic that he 'knew that the young officers were ready to show solidarity with the two generals if any sanctions were imposed on them.' The President of the Council showed Thomaz that he sensed that the most conservative sectors of the regime had already demanded the resignation of the two generals from the head of state. Pressure on Thomaz came from Kaúlza de Arriaga, who wrote a dramatic letter to the President of the Republic, expressing his apprehensions,[83] from ambassador Franco Nogueira, engineer Duarte Amaral and Admiral Henrique Tenreiro, who, in successive audiences, did not hide 'the enormity of the dangers.'[84]

These moves by the most conservative wing of the regime did not go unnoticed in diplomatic circles. On 7 March, the US State Department reported that Spínola's book had provoked a serious political crisis in Portugal and that Thomaz was demanding Spínola's resignation, having on his side the ministers of the Interior (Moreira Baptista), Defence (Silva Cunha) and the Army (Andrade e Silva), as well as personalities from the right-wing of the regime. Within these circles, it is thought that Caetano gave his agreement to the publication of the book, which was seen as a very serious matter. The pressure on Caetano was great and the State Department was already aware that the head of government was considering resigning and leaving the scene.[85]

In fact, the situation was 'extremely delicate' and Caetano even suggested to the President to accept the resignation of the executive, in order to try to form another government 'with greater freedom of movement and that would ward off the imminent danger.'[86] Although Thomaz never mentions this part of the hearing in his

The government, headed by Marcello Caetano, in the centre, congratulates the President of the Republic, Américo Thomaz, on the left, in white uniform, on his promotion to Admiral in 1970. Four years later, Caetano twice expressed his desire to leave power but Thomaz never accepted the head of government's resignation. (Museum of the Presidency)

memoirs, Caetano states that the President of the Republic replied that the exoneration did not make sense because it would throw the country into the unknown. Moreover, he felt that Caetano had the confidence of the Portuguese people and that he, Thomaz, had reason to keep it. Marcello, a legalist, interpreted that all that remained was for him to seek 'through constitutional means to obtain the expression of the will of the Nation.'[87] That is to say, in a flight to the front, to seek the regime's survival before public opinion, resorting to the National Assembly, which had to pronounce itself on the overseas policy being followed until then. With a parliament dominated by deputies belonging to the regime's party, it was easy to guess the result.

2
TORTUOUS PATHS

While preparing the performance to demonstrate to the country that governance was firm, Marcello Caetano faced failure on the external front trying to convince the United States of America (USA) to supply Portugal with arms. The regime's hopes of obtaining arms in exchange for the use of the Lajes base (Azores) by the USA during the Middle East conflict in October 1973, had faded.

The Syrian and Egyptian attack on Israel, with logistical and technical support from the Soviet Union, had taken place on 6 October 1973, during the religious holiday of Yom Kippur (Day of Forgiveness) in Israel and had left the Jewish state in a dramatic situation. Suffering a coordinated attack on two fronts, north and south, the Israelis took significant casualties in the early days of the war and military experts in Washington and Tel Aviv decided that a substantial strengthening of Israel's military arsenal was necessary. Moscow was heavily supporting Syria and Egypt with the transport of war material to these two countries and the US needed to do the same in relation to Israel. As the time factor was vital, only the intensive use of the Lajes base for aircraft refuelling would save the Israeli military forces from great difficulties, as all other bases situated in route to Israel were closed to American use.[1]

Lajes represented an important strategic point in the Atlantic and Marcello Caetano hoped to take some advantage of this in the relationship with the US. However, before the October war, the strategy followed in the State Department was to downplay the importance of the base, in order to be able to use it without paying a high price. This can be seen in a September 1973 memorandum from Thomas Pickering, Executive Secretary of the State Department, to Brent Scowcroft, Deputy Assistant to the President for National Security Affairs, warning that the Azores Agreement was expiring on 4 February 1974 (with a negotiation period until 4 August 1974) and that 'given the continuing strategic importance of the Lajes complex and its specific relevance to anti-submarine warfare in the Atlantic, a new agreement should be sought to extend our access to these facilities. In return, the Portuguese will want as high an economic and political price as possible.'[2]

In July 1973, the Secretary of State, William Rogers, had already had a preliminary conversation with the Portuguese Minister of Foreign Affairs, Rui Patrício, in Helsinki (Finland), in which he stressed the importance of the base facilities for the entire Atlantic Alliance. However, in that conversation, Rogers suggested that the base be made available without any kind of counterpart representing Portugal's contribution to Western defence, which Patrício disagreed with, as he hoped to negotiate the base on better terms.

Pickering suggested that the new Secretary of State, Henry Kissinger, should maintain this approach when he had the opportunity to talk to Rui Patrício and that this should be the strategy to be followed in talks with the Portuguese.[3] However, this strategy of devaluing Lajes changed with the Arab Israeli war.

The American request

Initially, Marcello Caetano hesitated to grant the Americans permission to pass through the Azores, as he feared reprisals from Arab countries. He was also dissatisfied with the lack of American support for the colonial issue, which translated into an embargo

Jewish troops carry wounded onto a Sikorsky S-65C-3 (CH-53D) of the Israel defence forces during the 1973 war. Israel had strong US support during this conflict through the Lajes base in the Azores. (IDF)

Richard Nixon and Marcello Caetano in 1971, during the summit that brought together, in the Azores, Nixon and French President Georges Pompidou. In the background, we can see the supersonic Concorde, which brought Pompidou to the Lajes base. (Richard Nixon Presidential Library)

on arms sales and the approval in Congress, of legislation hostile to Portuguese interests. Caetano knew US President Richard Nixon personally, as he had been with him in Lajes in December 1971, during a summit meeting in the Azores between Nixon and French President Georges Pompidou. At that time, the French leader arrived at Lajes in the supersonic Concorde, which was still in the experimental flight phase, but was a flag of France's prestige in the aeronautical sector. The meeting between Nixon and Pompidou was intended to discuss monetary policies, but Caetano took the opportunity to appear alongside the most powerful leaders of the Western world. The head of the Portuguese government had bilateral meetings with Nixon and Pompidou but got little out of it. The Portuguese regime remained isolated, and the Americans did not supply any arms to Portugal but the war between Israel and the Arabs created a new opportunity for Caetano to put pressure on Nixon.

Realising that the Americans could not help Israel without passing through the Azorean base, Caetano tried to obtain some dividends by showing little interest in authorising the passage of American transport planes through Lajes, without there being political and military counterparts.

The American request arrived on Friday 12 October from the American embassy in Lisbon, following a missive sent by the American Secretary of State, Henry Kissinger.[4] In Washington, the Portuguese ambassador, João Hall Themido, was informed at the State Department on the morning of the day of the request, to begin using the base that evening, and immediately expressed reservations as to the appropriateness of the request. For Themido, Portugal had good reason not to authorise the American request, as it felt disregarded by Richard Nixon's administration and did not

During the period of one month, the Americans delivered around 22,000 tons of military equipment to the Israelis, which was essential to contain the Arab offensive and save the Jewish state. (US archives)

want to harass Arab countries by getting involved in a war alongside Israel.[5] Themido's position was obviously supported in Lisbon and in the Ministry of Foreign Affairs, Rui Patrício, in agreement with Caetano, made the authorisation to use Lajes, dependent on concrete compensations in the political and military field.

Washington had no time for negotiations and Henry Kissinger lost patience with the Portuguese attitude and sent a letter to Lisbon, on behalf of President Nixon, threatening that Portugal would be left to its own destiny if it did not collaborate on this vital issue and that there would be consequences for Luso-American relations.[6] The letter was sent on 13 October (Saturday), at a time when Caetano was on a visit to the interior of the country and it was there that he coordinated a reply, by telephone, with Rui Patrício, who was in Lisbon. The message written by Kissinger was in fact, an ultimatum and Caetano realised that it was more advantageous to collaborate on the air bridge to Israel than to confront the United States. Portugal thus gave in to American pressure. On 14 October (Sunday), the first American cargo plane, a C-5 Galaxy, landed at Tel Aviv airport with military equipment. In the following 30 days, the Americans delivered around 22,000 tons of military equipment to the Israelis, which was essential to contain the Arab offensive and save the Jewish state and Portugal had been a precious ally in this strategy.[7]

It is interesting to note that a few days after this moment of tension between Lisbon and Washington, Caetano summoned the Supreme Council of National Defence to explain the strategy he had followed. The meeting took place on 19 October and the Council's president admitted that the US could have forced the use of Lajes, even without Portuguese authorisation: 'Which would make us lose any advantages, immediate or future, that a collaborative attitude might give us hope of obtaining.' Thus, he decided to allow the use of the Azorean base, making the US aware of 'the risks to which Portugal was subjected, which would justify the provision of means of defence (mainly missiles) emphasise the needs of our defence in the face of the increased threat.'[8] In fact, Caetano had sent a letter to Nixon on 19 October complaining that 'a campaign conducted by our enemies has deprived Portugal in recent years of effective means of military defence in Europe. The entire effort in the fight against subversion in Africa is being made with internal resources.' In the face of these difficulties, the US did nothing to help Portugal and Caetano even argued that 'Portuguese public opinion is today convinced that the United States abandons friendly countries even when the interests they defend coincide fundamentally with those of the West and, therefore, with American interests.'

For the Portuguese leader, the Soviet Union had a global strategic vision in which the conquest of positions in Africa was important to Moscow and Portugal, by fighting the African nationalist movements, which had the support of the Soviets, was going against this strategy of global domination. It was, therefore, important to have a more active collaboration between the USA and Portugal in defence of the interests of the West, at a time when the American Congress was voting for an arms embargo on Portugal. In Caetano's opinion, this attitude would always have negative effects on Portuguese public opinion and the Portuguese government's position.[9]

In search of missiles

At the time, Portugal was desperately trying to obtain portable surface-to-air missiles of the Redeye type[10] to protect Portuguese troops in Guinea, who could at any moment, be attacked by MiG-17 fighters coming from Guinea-Conakry. The issue was debated at the 19 October meeting of the CSDN, with the CEMGFA, Costa Gomes, making an analysis of the situation in the Overseas, in the period from May to the end of September 1973. He drew the attention of those present, to a possible escalation of the war in Guinea with the intervention of the Republic of Guinea, since that country had MiG-15 and MiG-17 fighters and there was information about PAIGC pilots being trained in the Soviet Union, who could join those of the Republic of Guinea's own Air Force. Costa Gomes also mentioned that the military situation in the colony had worsened due to the guerrillas' new military capabilities (the guerrillas had received long-range artillery and Strela surface-to-air missiles) and the change in the concept of manoeuvre that led the PAIGC to make large concentrations of forces around three Portuguese troop barracks in border areas, which it isolated and bombed with high firepower. As a result, lamented Costa Gomes: 'Our forces had 125 dead and 586 wounded by the end of the period under review, which are very high numbers (corresponding to the loss of a battalion), of which 96 dead and 500 wounded in the month of May alone,' when the attacks on the barracks had been most intense.

The situation could get even worse in the case of an air attack, which, in CEMGFA's opinion, could lead to the military collapse of the Portuguese forces in that theatre of operations. As such, he argued that the new threat required the existence of appropriate anti-aircraft defence means for Bissau, which would have to include surface-to-air missiles and complementarily, modern fighter planes (he referred to the Mirage), which could be used to retaliate against the neighbouring country.[11] The defence of Bissau was a priority but any barracks in Guinea could be attacked, which also required portable surface-to-air missiles to defend Portuguese troops, not only in Bissau, but eventually elsewhere in Guinea.

Few countries could supply the missiles Portugal needed and the steps taken so far to obtain them, had been unsuccessful.[12] The difficulties in acquiring war material were addressed in the meeting, with the Minister of Defence, Viana Rebelo, informing those present of the initiatives of national defence industries to produce new weapons such as rocket-propelled grenade launchers. He also told of the negotiations with South Africa for the supply of war material, some of which had already been supplied, such as artillery grenades and campaign tents. At this time, Pretoria was the great ally that Portugal had in the war in Africa and besides military equipment, there was the possibility of a considerable loan in money to re-equip the Portuguese forces that urgently needed to be modernised [13].

However, all this implied supplementary expenses which the Minister of Finance, Manuel Cota Dias, was not yet in a position to ensure without knowing the budget execution of the year in progress, recalling, however, that in the year in question (1973), the amount of extraordinary expenses had been high and could not be exceeded so as not to run the risk of unbalancing public accounts.[14] Moreover, it was clear that Portugal needed more money to re-equip the armed forces and also a greater understanding from the United States regarding the sale of armaments.

A US Army soldier aims an FIM-43C Redeye anti-aircraft guided missile system launcher during a training exercise in 1973. Portugal tried to obtain this missile from the US. (US National Archives)

A matter of life and death

After the Arab Israeli war, Portugal had lost out in its collaboration with Washington and Tel Aviv. The losses had been the nationalisation by the Baghdad government, of the shares of the Calouste Gulbenkian Foundation, resulting in a loss of three-quarters of its oil revenues; the severing of diplomatic relations with Lebanon and the embargo on oil products. Despite these losses, Portugal had not managed to break the arms embargo. However, the war in the Middle East had given the Azorean base a new geostrategic importance and the United States was now more

Portuguese ambassador João Hall Themido with Nixon and Kissinger at the White House in November 1973. (Richard Nixon Presidential Library)

Another view of the meeting between Themido and Nixon. During the meeting, Nixon showed understanding for the Portuguese policy in Africa, although he could not admit it publicly. (Richard Nixon Presidential Library)

US Secretary of State Henry Kissinger (right) met Portuguese foreign minister Rui Patrício at a Brussels hotel to thank Portugal for its support during the war in the Middle East. (AP)

interested in the renegotiation of the Azores Agreement which was expiring in February 1974.

Meanwhile, on 26 November 1973, the Portuguese ambassador João Hall Themido was received by Nixon at the White House in the presence of Kissinger. It was an affable meeting with Nixon thanking Portugal for its collaboration at a difficult time, when other allied countries preferred not to commit themselves. Themido took the opportunity to draw attention to the reprisals Portugal had suffered for collaborating with the USA and the need to receive defensive armaments, given the worsening military situation in Guinea. In this context, the arms embargo only benefited Portugal's enemies and could create a military imbalance with serious consequences in the African territories. Nixon was unaware of the difficulties the Portuguese were facing, which led Kissinger to intervene to say that they could supply the missiles Portugal wanted through a third country, in order to avoid criticism from Congress. Nixon agreed with this possibility and was even sympathetic to Portuguese colonial policy, which he considered to be an internal Portuguese matter but he could not say so publicly, due to an American black community that was hostile to Portugal, in addition to the opposition he had in Congress. In this regard, Kissinger stated that he was trying to change Congress's attitude towards Portugal and that he had given the State Department guidelines to follow a political line more favourable to Portuguese interests and that he would talk about these and other problems during the visit he was planning to make to Lisbon in mid-December.[15]

Meanwhile, in early December, Rui Patrício had the opportunity to speak with Kissinger on the sidelines of a meeting with NATO (North Atlantic Treaty Organisation) ministers in Brussels. The meeting took place on 9 December and Kissinger agreed to speak with Patrício to thank him for Portugal's collaboration during the Arab Israeli war. The Portuguese minister thanked him for the deference and stressed the key role Portugal had played in supplying Israel. He stated that Arab countries were aware of this and that the country now urgently needed defensive military equipment, notably surface-to-air missiles, to protect itself from a possible military escalation in Guinea, which could involve air strikes against Bissau in January 1974 and that Portuguese forces had no effective weapon against such attacks. In response, Kissinger reiterated the importance of the Azores base to the US administration and that the State Department had orders not to cause political problems to Portugal. During the conversation, Patrício said he was not trying to market the Lajes base, but only to show Kissinger a vital problem of survival for Portugal. If the situation in Guinea ended in a military disaster, this could have unforeseeable consequences in Portugal, leading eventually to the fall of the regime and the arrival in power of leftist forces. This would advocate another overseas policy, as well as Portugal's withdrawal from NATO and consequently, from the Azores. Therefore, for the Portuguese leader, it was a matter of life or death.

During the meeting, Kissinger was sympathetic to the need for the Portuguese to have the missiles but said that a direct supply was impossible because of opposition from the US Congress. However, he committed himself to trying to find an alternative solution, which could involve Israel, something that had been suggested to the Portuguese authorities before. In this regard, Patrício replied that the Portuguese ambassador in Washington had not yet managed to talk to his Israeli counterpart, but Kissinger replied that he knew that the Israeli ambassador would receive João Hall Themido shortly.[16]

The day after this meeting, on 10 December, Themido met his Israeli colleague in the American capital, ambassador Simcha Dinitz. The Israeli diplomat apologised for not having been able to receive Themido earlier, as he had been very busy and most of the time absent but thanked him very much for his support during the war in the Middle East. Themido explained that he had contacted Dinitz on the advice of the American government to inquire about the possibility of Israel supplying Portugal with surface-to-air missiles against aircraft flying at medium and low altitudes. Dinitz replied that he would be happy to help, but that he was not sure what kind of missiles Israel could provide. Although he was not a military technician, his impression was that Israel had Hawk missiles, but did not know if they could be sold because they were of American origin.[17] He did, however, undertake to look into the matter with the Israeli government by asking Themido to tell him the number and type of missiles he wanted.[18]

A Hawk missile battery during the Yom Kippur war when Israel was attacked by its Arab neighbours. (IDF)

President Nixon receiving diplomatic credentials from the incoming ambassador from the State of Israel Simcha Dinitz in September 1973. It was Dinitz who spoke to Themido in Washington, DC. (Richard Nixon Presidential Library)

In response to this last question, Lisbon sent Washington, on 13 December, a list of material in which it asked for the following: Hawk missiles,[19] (a training unit, six double platoons and ammunition); Redeye missiles (1,000 missiles); modern vehicles with mounted anti-tank systems (a training unit + vehicles + 200/300 systems).[20] That same day, Themido talked to the chargé d'affaires of the Israeli embassy, who told him that Tel Aviv could only supply the missiles the Portuguese wanted with American authorisation, thus barring any chance of Israel serving as a transit country for American weapons destined for Portugal.[21]

Dissatisfied with the reply, Themido received instructions from Lisbon to speak at the State Department with William Porter, Under-Secretary of State for Political Affairs, who had suggested the meeting between the Portuguese ambassador and the Israeli diplomat.[22] On 15 December, Themido met with Porter and the latter told him that he had only suggested to the Israeli ambassador that, in contact with Themido, he should find out about the availability of war material and the possibility of supply, but without going into details. Later, in two telephone calls to the Portuguese embassy, Porter even says that in his contacts with Dinitz, he had only told

President Nixon seated informally in his office during a meeting with William Porter, US ambassador to the Paris peace negotiations in August 1971. A few years later, Porter would be the State Department's chief negotiator with the Portuguese. (Richard Nixon Presidential Library)

him that Portugal was interested in acquiring surface-to-air missiles but did not address any possibility of Tel Aviv supplying US missiles to Portugal; this left Themido disappointed with Porter's attitude. At the time, a Portuguese military mission was due to arrive in the American capital on 18 December (the day Henry Kissinger was in Lisbon) to discuss the arms Portugal wanted within the framework of the renegotiation of the Azores Agreement. On this issue, Porter hesitated and even told Themido in the first telephone call, that the immediate arrival of the mission in Washington might not lead to positive results, but in a second telephone call, he backed down and declared that the mission should go to the US as planned.[23] The armament the Portuguese requested is in a memorandum, in English and was delivered to Kissinger on 17 December 1973, when he passed through Lisbon after a visit to the Middle East.[24]

Kissinger in Lisbon

Kissinger landed in Lisbon on 17 December 1973 in the late afternoon for a 22-hour trip on Portuguese soil, continuing on 18 December to Madrid (Spain) to meet General Francisco Franco and Prince Juan Carlos. On the day he arrived, Kissinger had dinner at the Palácio das Necessidades, invited by Rui Patrício and after the meal, he had a restricted meeting with his Portuguese colleague attended by the Portuguese ambassador to the US, João Hall Themido, and the Director General of Political Affairs of the Ministry of Foreign Affairs, ambassador João de Freitas Cruz. On the American side there was Richard Post, chargé d'affaires of the American Embassy in Lisbon and Peter Rodman, of the National Security Council, who accompanied Kissinger on the visit.

During the conversation, Patrício drew attention to the war Portugal was fighting in Africa, which was no longer just a guerrilla war, as it could at any moment, involve foreign conventional forces. For this reason, the Portuguese minister was asking for 'defensive weapons' that would allow the country to defend itself 'against the attack of a foreign intervention army.' In response, Kissinger mentioned that the US was prepared to explore with the Portuguese the possibility of supplying arms, but without any publicity. This led Patrício to say that Portugal would be prepared for a secret agreement, if necessary and then showed a memorandum he had prepared to deliver to Kissinger with the Portuguese demands. The memorandum states:

I The Agreement will be a political document: its text will only mention political points.

II There will also be with the same force, an agreement for the supply of defensive equipment by the USA to Portugal. It will include only a few items, but all of them of capital importance and of the same first priority. Pending US and Portuguese experts' advice for exact types and quantities, it is already possible to assess our requirements as follows:

Surface-to-air missiles

1 Hawk type for the defence of 3 points:

- Guinea (planes and bombs in the hands of terrorists; Soviet presence increasing; fighters and long-range reconnaissance planes)
- Cabinda, Angola (oil installations: US sources had already passed information regarding possible attacks)
- Cabora-Bassa, Mozambique (very important power plant over the Zambeze)

Quantities: One Training Unit, 6 Double Platoons, Ammunitions

Redeye Type (Individual Missile. Very Accurate. Terrorists Armed With Redeye Are Being Court-Martialled For Failure To Shoot Down Aircraft.[25])

Quantity: 1,000 Rounds Of Ammunition

Kissinger's meeting in Lisbon with Rui Patrício on December 17, 1973. (Yale University Library)

Modern Vehicle-Mounted Anti-Tank Systems

Quantity: One Training Unit: 100 Vehicles – 200/300 Systems
For A) And B) Should Be Ensured The Supply Of Spare Parts And Ammunition. The Present Void Of Adequate Defensive Equipment Invites attacks.
III – C-130 and Orion planes. There is an acute need for transport aircraft: C-130s.
Quantity: 4
For the patrol and rescue squadron (also employed in ASW), to be based in the Azores, the Orion is the most suitable aircraft.

Quantity: 4
They will be used for NATO missions.
IV – Sea-to-air missiles. The oil platform in Cabinda is at sea. The presence of some naval units equipped with missiles will provide a strong deterrent and also a strong defence, both in Cabinda and at other vital points.

Quantity: 10 (to be applied on frigates or missile boats)

After reading the document, Kissinger acknowledged 'that an agreement of this magnitude cannot easily be done in secret' and that he had to study the request to see what could be provided. He promised an answer within a month of his return to Washington. Kissinger agreed with Patrício that a guerrilla war is one thing, attack by a land army is another, but that it would not be easy to supply the arms Portugal wants because of Congress. In this regard, the Portuguese minister suggested that 'now that Congress has approved huge aid to Israel, perhaps Israel could divert some to us.' 'Maybe that could be done,' Kissinger replies and promises that he will talk to the Israeli ambassador when he returns to the US. At this part of the conversation, Freitas Cruz intervened to say that there may have been some misunderstanding with the Israelis, given the failure of the contacts that Themido made in Washington with ambassador Simcha Dinitz. Freitas Cruz reported that the Israelis said they might be able to supply some surface-to-air missiles that they captured from the other side during the war and Kissinger agreed that would be a good way to do it. 'In fact, their SAMs (Surface-Air-Missile) are as good or better than the Hawk' and promised to look into the matter.[26]

The day after the departure of the head of American diplomacy, on 19 December, Diário de Lisbon headlined: 'The results of Kissinger's visit are unknown.' Neither the US Secretary of State nor the Portuguese Minister of Foreign Affairs made any statements to the national and foreign press at the end of the visit. A joint communiqué (United States and Portugal) was released about the meeting, reporting that Kissinger was received by the President of the Republic, Américo Thomaz and had talks with the President of the Council, Marcello Caetano. The same statement also said that the US Secretary of State and the Portuguese minister, 'had the opportunity to address the most important problems of the international situation at the present time, and bilateral relations between the United States and Portugal were fully examined.'

The visit was widely photographed and covered in the Lisbon press, which immediately reported the arrival of a 'smiling' Kissinger on the tarmac as he was welcomed by Rui Patrício. The press then highlighted Patrício's welcome statements in English, during which he reinforced that 'Portugal has been a good and faithful friend of the United States.' For his part, Kissinger stated that Portugal 'has

During his time in Lisbon Kissinger also met with Caetano. (Yale University Library)

stood firmly by its allies during the recent difficulties and the United States is extremely grateful for that.'

The national press also wrote that after these declarations, a meeting took place in São Bento with Caetano, that lasted 50 minutes. After this meeting, a working dinner followed at the Palácio das Necessidades with the Portuguese counterpart, as well as ambassadors Calvet de Magalhães, Freitas Cruz, Hall Themido and Tomás Andersen and also General Câmara Pina, director of the National Defence Institute. On the American side, besides Kissinger, were Richard Post, Chargé d'Affaires and five assistants to the Secretary of State. The following day, the American leader met with the President of the Republic in Belém and held new talks with Rui Patrício. Portugal offered him lunch at Queluz and on the way there, he stopped at Jerónimos Monastery, the Monument to the Discoveries and Belém Tower.

In the foreign press it was possible to better understand the real reasons for the visit with reports that Portugal would be interested in asking Kissinger for weapons, as the *Rand Daily Mail* wrote from Pretoria (South Africa), adding that the Portuguese government would ask for the supply of sophisticated weaponry to deal with the Soviet weapons used in the Portuguese territories in Africa. It also wrote that Portugal would try to renew the contract for the Lajes Base in the Azores.

Le Monde (France) wrote that Kissinger was extremely grateful to Portugal for its help in the October war and citing sources in Washington, said that Portugal wanted improved weapons to defend itself against Soviet material used by the nationalist resistance in Angola, Mozambique and Guinea-Bissau, and commented that the possibility of satisfying these requests was viewed with scepticism in the American capital.

The American *Washington Star News* wrote that Kissinger intended to express his gratitude for the way Portugal supported the United States in the Middle East war (facilities granted by the Azores military base). Referring to the welcome ceremonies on arrival at the airport, the newspaper writes that Kissinger said he came to thank Portugal on behalf of the American President, Richard Nixon and called Portugal 'a good and reliable friend of the United States,' although he did not mention that other NATO allies denied the US refuelling. According to the newspaper, Patrício replied that Portugal admired the American people.

As for concrete results from the visit to Portugal, given that the Lajes Base agreement was due to expire in just two months, the newspaper said that the Secretary of State was anxious to establish a general agreement on the conditions for its renewa,l since the Azores had proved essential in the Middle East war when the British, Germans, Italians, Greeks and Turks refused to cooperate for fear of problems with oil exports. In the newspaper's analysis, for Portugal, it was important to strengthen ties with the United States because of the animosity against the Lisbon regime on the part of Arabs, black Africa and third world nations. Also because Portugal was fighting guerrilla forces in its three African territories and was under constant attack in the United Nations from third world countries and the Warsaw Pact, due to colonialism [27].

Disillusionment

The memorandum delivered to Kissinger was analysed by the State Department and certainly by the Pentagon, but the Portuguese minister was anxious for a rapid response and in Lisbon, put pressure on the American ambassador Nash Scott. In a meeting he had with the latter on 16 January, the minister radicalised the Portuguese complaints. 'The ties between the two countries were only one-sided': from Portugal to the United States. Rui Patrício recalled the support given to America in the Middle East conflict and that the consequences of that support had been more serious for Portugal. He alluded to the fact that three weeks had passed since Kissinger's visit to Lisbon and there was still no response to the requests made for arms aid for the war in Africa. In this sense, he said that he was pessimistic about the renewal of the agreement on the American use of the Lajes base. He also reported that Scott reiterated that the requests were being studied.[28]

In fact, the American ambassador told him that they were complex matters, which also involved the attitude of the American Congress and that as soon as possible, a response would be given. Patrício replied that Congress should understand that at certain times, it is necessary to take difficult decisions that may displease some countries and that the United States could not treat trusted friends, such as Portugal, the same way as other countries. Scott then recalled that the US was a good friend of Portugal, when this is increasingly rare and that the Lajes base was important for both countries.[29]

However, the response from the American capital turned out to be a huge disappointment for the Portuguese government. On 8 February 1974, Assistant Secretary of State, Kenneth Rush called the Portuguese ambassador to the State Department to tell him that the US could not supply the Redeye missiles because they were in talks with Moscow to limit the spread of Man-Portable Air Defence Systems (MANPADS), as was the case with those missiles and, moreover, the missiles 'would be used domestically in the fight against guerrillas, which was unacceptable.' The same was true of vehicles with anti-tank systems, which could not be supplied either since they were to be used in Africa. Regarding the Hawk missiles, they would have to consult Congress, if Portugal agreed to this consultation. The same was true for the missiles for ships in which Portugal was interested. Less problematic was the transfer of the P-3 Orion aircraft, which Rush thought would be possible. Themido then asked him what the American position was regarding the C-130 transport planes, with Rush arguing that they could not be supplied either, as they would be used to transport troops to Africa. The Portuguese ambassador also asked him about the possibility of arms being supplied by a third country, but Rush said that such a possibility would not avoid problems with Congress.

Themido returned to the embassy disbelieving in any kind of military aid and transmitted this disappointment to Lisbon in the telegram he sent to the Ministry of Foreign Affairs that same day.[30] Rui Patrício lost no time and prepared a tough response, which included breaking off negotiations with the Americans if there were no significant compensations. On 7 March, the minister himself wrote a letter to Henry Kissinger contesting the American position and expressing his deep disappointment at the decision not to supply the arms Portugal needed to defend itself in Africa.[31] Shortly afterwards, he instructed Themido (who had been in Lisbon) to go to Rush and inform him of Portugal's intention not to renew the American presence in Lajes.[32] The minister hoped that this position of strength would lead the Americans to give in and provide military aid at a decisive moment for the country when there were fears of external intervention in the Portuguese colonies.

The nuclear power plants

On 18 March, the Portuguese ambassador went to the State Department and showed Rush a statement in which the Portuguese government ended the facilities the US had at the Azorean base.[33] Rush did not hide his astonishment at the Portuguese intention but reaffirmed that the USA had an interest in maintaining the base and good relations with Portugal. Themido replied that there could only be an agreement if there were substantial compensations and that the US was unnecessarily dragging out negotiations when the time factor was crucial to Portugal. He gave as an example, the response to the December memorandum, which had been negative and which had taken over two months, when it could have been quicker. Rush explained that the delay in the response had to do with the fact that all possible ways to supply the requested material had been explored and studied, but that this had not been possible, given that in military aid, they were very limited by Congress. However, they could help in other fields and produced a proposal of a nuclear plant.[34] The suggestion was surprising, given that Portugal had no experience in the field of nuclear power stations.

Themido left the meeting relatively satisfied and on 20 March, wrote to Lisbon advising Patrício not to renew the request for armaments which he saw as impossible to fulfil, however, he thought that one should insist on C-130s which could be sold in their civilian version, to a Portuguese airline and could then be rented by the State to perform missions in Africa. In addition, Themido considered that the following items should be requested as compensation:

- General political support, as already indicated.
- 4 Orion aircraft;
- 4 C-130 aircraft
- Sonar equipment, as requested in due course.
- Supply and installation of a nuclear power station.
- Scholarships worth $1 million;
- Supply of cereals up to a limit of US$ 15 million in each year of validity of the Agreement.
- Technical and financial collaboration in the prospection and possible use of geothermal energy in the Azores.

From this list, Themido considered that the most important point was the nuclear power station and that the request for the power station should be presented more precisely, after consultation with Portuguese technicians. In the remaining requests, there could be some concessions during the negotiations since they were relatively modest.[35]

Meanwhile, on 11 April, Kissinger replied to Patrício that any supply of military equipment to Portugal, had to have the approval of Congress and that this approval could not be taken for granted.

The old Lockheed P2V-5 Neptune, which Portugal used during the 1960s and 1970s, needed to be replaced but the country was never able to buy the P-3 Orion. The Portuguese Air Force had to wait until the late 1980s to receive the first P-3s. (NATO Collection)

He therefore suggested cooperation in other non-military areas that would benefit all segments of Portuguese society and maintained his interest in renewing the Azores Agreement.[36]

Although the letter makes no reference to the missiles Portugal wanted so badly, the truth was that Kissinger managed to obtain their supply by tortuous means. Taking advantage of the fact that Israel was receiving large quantities of arms after the October war, Kissinger allegedly convinced the Israelis to divert 500 Redeye missiles from their stock and send them to Portugal through a German intermediary. The number of missiles ordered shows that the Redeye were not only intended for Guinea, where Portuguese forces needed about 200 missiles, but also for other points in the Portuguese colonies. The missiles had already arrived in Germany when the April 25th revolution took place and the regime fell.[37] The new government decided then to suspend the shipment of the missiles, although as can be seen from a communication of July 1974 from the General Secretariat of National Defence (SGDN)[38], the possible shipment of the missiles to the Overseas Territories was still being questioned. At that time, in a reply to a note from the Army Staff (EME – *Estado-Maior do Exército*), an officer of the 1st Division of the SGDN suggested that 'at the level of the EMGFA (*Estado-Maior General das Forças Armadas* – Armed Forces General Staff) a decision should be taken whether or not to send the missiles to the Overseas. In the affirmative case, consult the Commanders-in-Chief of the respective TO (Theatres of Operations) about which posts should be protected by these weapons.' The missiles were to be assigned according to the 'geographical location of the units, whether or not they are within range of potentially enemy air assets, and to considerations of importance of the objectives, whether or not they are remunerative for an air attack.'[39]

Rui Patrício still had knowledge about the outcome of the missiles, as contained in a letter he wrote to João Hall Themido, on April 23 and which was never delivered (it was retained at the ministry), he informs the diplomat (who already had verbal knowledge) of contacts made 'by a private entity with the Department of National Defence which are of the utmost importance,' although he admits not to have 'sufficient elements to assess the true origin of this initiative and its effective possibility of implementation.' Although he does not reveal the exact content of this initiative, it appears to be about the missiles, since the minister instructs Themido to resume talks with the State Department, a sign that the disagreements that led to the suspension of the negotiations had been overcome, although he advised Themido not to make any reference to the missiles in his contacts with the Americans.

For the Portuguese minister, the priority becomes the nuclear power plant as can be seen in an annex to the letter, containing the detailed plans for the implementation of a nuclear power plant in Portugal, indicating the investments to be made and their phasing in time.[40] In essence, Patrício followed the recommendations that Themido had given on 20 March not insisting on the request for military material, except for the 4 C-130 aircrafts, which could be provided in their civilian version. Regarding the P-3 Orion, he considered that they should also be requested, but with a lesser degree of importance, given that these planes would be dedicated to maritime patrol missions within the scope of the Atlantic Alliance. However, they were important aircraft to replace the old Lockheed P2V-5 Neptune, which Portugal used in maritime missions and which were already outdated. Patrício also considered it important to know what kind of support the Americans could provide in the event of foreign military intervention in the Portuguese colonies.[41] On the other side of the Atlantic, the answer would never come.

3
THE SITUATION IN THE COLONIES

While the regime negotiated at different levels and results were slow to appear, in the theatre of operations, Marcello Caetano was still confronted with the worsening situation in Mozambique in early 1974. In the colony, the white population was dissatisfied with the performance of the military, after an attack on 14 January on a family of white farmers by FRELIMO guerrillas in the Manica area, near the border with Rhodesia. In this attack, the wife of a rural landowner was killed and the episode provoked strong reactions among the white population, which did not expect to see war in this region. Outraged by the situation, the white shopkeepers of Vila Pery (Chimoio), Vila Manica and Machipanda, decreed a general protest until the government gave them guarantees of security. This protest extended to the city of Beira, on the Indian Ocean coast. In this town, on 17 January, the Trade Association held a day of mourning for the death of the farmer's wife. During that day, moves began to happen in the city and in the evening, hundreds of people showed their anger near the army officers' mess hall, accusing them of easy living and cowardice. Some of the more exalted people threw stones at the building and fired pistol shots. The protests were eventually repressed by the military police who were on the scene, but it was clear that the white population was dissatisfied with the efficiency of the Portuguese troops.[1]

The unease was notorious and some elements of the captains' movement in Mozambique wrote a protest to be delivered to the CEMGFA, Costa Gomes, signed by 180 officers of the military garrisons of Beira and Nampula, asking for 'the immediate resignation of the civil governor of Beira and other authorities (…) responsible for the maintenance of public order.'[2]

At that time, Costa Gomes had been sent by Marcello Caetano to Mozambique to assess the situation on the ground. The CEMGFA would travel to this province a few hours after attending the ceremony in which Spínola took up his duties as Vice-CEMGFA on 17 January. Costa Gomes arrived in the city of Beira on 18 January. In the following days, he travelled to Tete province in the interior of Mozambique, then to Nampula in the north and ended his visit in Lourenço Marques, the capital of Mozambique. During his 14-day stay in the colony (he returned on 1 February and then travelled on to Angola), Costa Gomes had the opportunity to make a detailed diagnosis of the situation, which resulted in a long report on the visit.[3]

During his time in Beira, Costa Gomes was monitored by Jorge Jardim, former under-secretary of State for Trade and Industry during the Salazar era and one of the most influential men in Mozambique. According to Jorge Jardim, the protests were promoted by a white activist minority, not representative of the Portuguese community.[4] With his influence in the colony, Jardim prevented the protests from gaining dimension and criticised the agitators, who ended up demobilising.[5] However, the protests caused unease among the Portuguese military forces who felt outraged.

Costa Gomes in Mozambique

The panorama that Costa Gomes found in Mozambique was not encouraging in relation to the conduct of the war, with the worsening of the military situation in the north and the attempted expansion of the guerrillas to the south.

FRELIMO's propaganda poster. Besides the guerrillas, the poster shows the Salazar's boat led by Marcello Caetano, about to sink. (Yale University Library)

A FRELIMO artillery unit carrying a mortar in Mozambique. Guerrilla units frequently bombard Portuguese army military posts in the colony. (AP)

Upon arriving in the colony, Costa Gomes found that the city of Beira was still in a state of great unrest due to the attack on the farmers' family in Manica. The day he arrived in the city, the crowd tried to hold another protest in front of the army mess hall but was prevented from doing so by the heavy police presence, which forced the crowd to disperse. During his two weeks in Mozambique, Costa Gomes held several meetings with civil and military authorities, who reported on the difficulties in controlling the guerrillas.

A FRELIMO guerrilla unit set up mortar, equipped with shoulder harness, for an attack against a Portuguese position. (AP)

At the end of the visit, on 30 January, he took part in a meeting of the Council of Defence of Mozambique, in which the governor himself, Manuel Pimentel dos Santos, admitted that FRELIMO was very strong in the region of Cabo Delgado, in the extreme northeast of the colony, where 'it began to act in large groups on objectives of great interest.' He asked Costa Gomes what the strategy should be, 'under the political point of view, to avoid the creation of conditions favourable to the declaration of independence.' The governor recalled what had happened in Guinea with the declaration of independence by the PAIGC in September 1973. Costa Gomes acknowledged that this way of acting by the guerrillas was not new and that it was already the case in 1966, when Costa Gomes had been in Mozambique with command responsibilities.

At that time, the barracks were the preferred targets and the best way to respond to this was a well-organised defence of the barracks with well-trained troops to cause heavy casualties to the guerrillas when they attacked. This implied, in addition, the need for good links between the land and air forces and not having small detachments of troops that could easily be annihilated. On the issue of independence, Costa Gomes was aware that nothing could be done to prevent it but argued that it was important to have mobile forces that could quickly reach any point in the territory and prevent the establishment of a FRELIMO government in Mozambique. With the agreement of the head of PIDE/DGS present at the meeting, he also stated that the best forces to interdict the border areas were the GE (Grupos Especiais – Special Groups) and the Flechas, composed of black troops, because they knew the terrain and had a better sense of direction and greater speed of march than regular troops. The Flechas were special operations units trained and supported by PIDE/DGS to carry out clandestine operations against insurgent movements. The special groups were constituted by Blacks who had been specially trained for counter-guerrilla operations. They were well-prepared troops who operated in small groups and were well-versed in the terrain

Another area where the Portuguese had problems was in the exact location of enemy bases in which the information did not always hit the mark or had location errors too high to take tactical advantage. On this issue, Costa Gomes recognised the problem, which could only be solved in two ways: through aerial photographic reconnaissance or with good guides. 'Without the help of these two elements looking for an enemy barrack is looking for the needle in a haystack.' Another hypothesis was radiolocation, but the Portuguese did not yet have the equipment.[6]

Another point discussed at the meeting was the hamleting of the native population, which needed to be done with great care and with the concern to give the population better socio-economic conditions than those they had previously.

Meeting at the Chief Command in Nampula in December 1973, when the Minister for Overseas, Baltazar Rebelo de Sousa, visited the colony. Rebelo de Sousa is in the centre of the photo (wearing glasses), with by his side, Mozambique's commander-in-chief, General Bastos Machado (in uniform) and the colony's governor, Manuel Pimentel dos Santos. (AHU)

The hamlets were also a way to better control the population, but it had to be done voluntarily and without coercion. Costa Gomes also stressed that a counter-subversion plan had to be very well coordinated between all civilian and military structures, down to the village level. Another important issue was information, which had to be harmonised between the various entities in order to be efficient.[7]

Another point discussed at the meeting was the delay in supplying arms to the security forces, with Mozambique's secretary-general, Teixeira Ferreira, complaining of two-year delays in meeting police requests. Costa Gomes confirmed the difficulties due to Portugal's dependence on foreign countries which prevented the sale of arms which could be used in Africa. Portugal only produced automatic rifles and light machine guns under licence, in addition to 60 and 81mm mortars, but Portuguese production was not enough to meet the needs of the armed forces, hence the difficulties in meeting the requests of other entities such as the police forces. As he did not agree with this situation, Costa Gomes had already agreed with the Minister of Defence that the police forces would be given a different kind of attention, with three-year timetables for the acquisition of weapons so that requests could be met in a timely manner.

A further problem was the lack of army officers to command the police. At this level, Costa Gomes painted a worrying picture. The troops in the Overseas Territories and in training in the metropolis, had approximately 200,000 men and according to that number, there should be 18,000 officers. In reality, there were little more than 4,000, which made it impossible to meet the needs of the police (which had a total of 24,000 men) and the armed forces. The salary increases that central government had recently promoted in the armed forces could possibly lead to a greater adherence to the permanent staff, although Costa Gomes was not sure about this, suggesting that militia officers should be invited for command functions in the police.[8]

Lack of officers

This problem denoted the enormous lack of officers in the Army's permanent staff, which was a cause for concern in the command of units in Africa. A study by the SGDN (General Secretariat of National Defence) dated March 1973, already drew attention to the problem, stating that it was a pressing issue and that officers in combat functions were reaching the threshold of exhaustion. The study showed that the number of officers the Army should have in the Metropolitan Region, in Overseas Territories and in reserve for the security forces, was far below what was necessary. In theory, there should be 5,650 officers in total, but in January 1972, there were only 2,875, that is, about half of the officers needed. Moreover, the shortages were more serious at the level of captains and non-commissioned officers, who were essential to command the overseas troops.

This shortage forced most officers to conduct various commissions in Africa without the necessary time to recover, which caused great wear and tear on the military, with physical and psychological exhaustion, as well as family problems of various kinds. These problems also extended to the sergeants, who were ageing, poorly educated and exhausted by consecutive mobilisations for the war in Africa. In its conclusions, the study warned of the extremely serious and potentially dangerous situation in the Army and of the need to take urgent and fundamental measures, so as not to run the risk of the Army collapsing, which would have serious social and political consequences.[9]

Defence Minister Viana Rebelo and Spínola. Rebelo tried to solve the problem of the lack of officers in the Portuguese Army but created an even bigger problem by trying to facilitate the access of militia officers to the permanent staff. (Revista do Povo collection)

Although it made a correct analysis of the problem, the study did not question the war and defended solutions that included making the military career more attractive with the valorisation of the courses at the Military Academy, the passage to the reserve after 20 years of service, an improvement in salaries, bonuses and social support, as well as rapid progression in the military hierarchy for the best and most dedicated. It is interesting to note that a few months after this study, the Minister of Defence, Viana Rebelo, tried to solve the problem by facilitating the access of militia officers to the permanent staff, which did not exactly correspond to a valorisation of the Military Academy courses.

Costa Gomes returned to Lisbon in the first week of February (after passing through Angola) and upon arriving in the Portuguese capital, said that the purpose of the visit to Angola and Mozambique was to make direct contact with civil and military authorities in those territories so that 'some measures to improve' the 'counter-subversion effort' could be 'studied together.'[10]

After his return to Portugal, Costa Gomes tried to keep up-to-date with the problems affecting Mozambique and on 8 February, he had a meeting, together with the Minister of Defence, with an official Navy chaplain, João Soares Cabeçadas, who had undergone religious service in Mozambique some years before. It was the minister himself who asked Cabeçadas to go to Mozambique and give news of what was happening there. In the middle of the month, the chaplain arrived in Beira from Lisbon and tried to contact some officers and civilians he knew in Mozambique. He found out that in Vila Manica, a 'black hunt' was going on, in his words, with armed settlers and the connivance of elements of the PIDE/DGS. In this context, about 200 Blacks had been arrested and of these, it was not known how many were still alive.

This explains a slogan attributed to the whites of Manica: 'We don't need the army and leave us with the DGS.' Mendes Cabeçadas

In 1974, after five years as Portugal's governor and military commander in Guinea, General Spínola was appointed Vice-Chief of Staff of the Armed Forces (Vice-CEMGFA). That February, Spínola, disillusioned by the regime's Overseas policy, published a book proclaiming the impossibility of a military victory in Portugal's colonial wars. Spínola's public candour in defiance of regime dogma, led to his dismissal and a failed military revolt led by officers loyal to him. In this image, taken during the Overseas War era, Spínola appears with his trademark swagger stick, decorations, gloves, and Prussian-style monocle. His uniform, although cut from the Portuguese Army's standard 'lizard' camouflage fabric, appears personally tailored, which was rather typical among senior officers of the time. He is wearing a canvas belt, but no weapons, and sports a 'Bigeard' style field cap (known as a 'quico' in Portugal). (Artwork by Anderson Subtil)

During the African wars, the Portuguese Navy's small Marine Corps maintained several detachments in the overseas colonies of Guinea, Angola and Mozambique. Portugal's Marines were divided between Special Marine Detachments (DFE) dedicated to amphibious assault and counter-guerrilla operations, and Marine Fusiliers Companies (CFN) employed primarily to protect naval vessels and installations. This Marine, serving in one of the Guinea-based DFEs, wears a modified M963 camouflage uniform. This uniform, based on a design worn by French paratroopers during their Indochina War, featured several modifications including a darker camouflage pattern better suited to African operations. Even in combat, the Fuzileiros were distinguished by a black beret with an anchor badge and the wear of naval rank insignia. (Artwork by Anderson Subtil)

Badge of the DFE 12. (Artwork by Anderson Subtil)

This native volunteer, in the typical Portuguese forces' resting position, is wearing the black uniform usually worn by Special Groups in Mozambique, although they also appeared in standard 'lizard' camouflage. He carries the yellow and white SG badge over the left shirt pocket, and two short bars at the top of the sleeve replace the Regular Forces' epaulet stripes. These units also adopted an unofficial yellow beret, clearly reserved for ceremonial functions and barracks duty. In the field, however, SG personnel wore the standard 'quico' cap in the 2-G pattern. An American pattern M56 canvas belt, a kerchief, and coloured boot laces – clearly parade accessories – complete the outfit. The weapon depicted is the widely used H&K G3 7.62mm NATO assault rifle, which was developed in West Germany at the time and produced under licence in Portugal. (Artwork by Anderson Subtil)

A soldier from the Popular Army for the Liberation of Angola (EPLA), the MPLA's military force, as he appeared at Luanda Airport during the mass exodus of Portuguese settlers in 1975. He is wearing a khaki uniform based on the Soviet 'tropical' pattern, including a hat of the same colour. His boots and carrier bag are also of Soviet or other Warsaw Pact origin, but the canvas belt is Portuguese Army issue, and the accessory bag seems to be of civilian origin. His weapon is an AK-47 assault rifle with a calibre of 7.62x39mm; more precisely, it is a Romanian model, easily recognised by the addition of a vertical grip on the front. (Artwork by Anderson Subtil)

The military arm of the PAIGC, the Revolutionary Armed Forces of the People (FARP), was the most effective insurgent force opposing Portuguese colonial rule. This illustration reflects the influence of Communist bloc military aid to African rebel movements. In addition to the Kalashnikov AK-47 assault rifle, which replaced obsolete Portuguese bolt-action rifles and PPSh-41 submachine guns, he is wearing olive green trousers, a camouflage shirt of Romanian origin and Soviet 'tropical' uniform belt and headgear. He is also wearing one of the CHICOM-style magazine rigs made famous by the Vietcong, fastened to the side of his waist rather than wrapped around his torso (the latter being more typical in Southeast Asia). (Artwork by Anderson Subtil)

The image depicts a young Portuguese conscript photographed on the streets of Lisbon on April 25, 1974, during the Armed Forces' Movement coup against the *Estado Novo* regime. He is dressed in the olive-green service uniform adopted in 1966, complete with black leather boots and the distinctive 'quico' cap, a local variation of the French 'Bigeard' style field cap. He wears a long raincoat made of synthetic material over his basic uniform, as well as distinctly Portuguese accoutrements such as braces and a canvas belt, although his ammunition pouches and canteen are missing. His weaponry consists of a 7.62mm NATO G3 assault rifle produced under Portuguese license by the Braço de Prata factory, which was itself located in a northeast Lisbon neighbourhood. (Artwork by Anderson Subtil)

Overseas air defence requirements led Portugal to request a delivery of Hughes MIM-23 HAWK (Homing All-the-Way Killer) surface-to-air missiles from the US in 1973-74. The issue was raised repeatedly during negotiations over continued American use of the Lajes air base, but Washington consistently equivocated, citing logistical and political obstacles. Had Portugal acquired the HAWK, it would have been deployed to protect strategic points in Guinea and Angola. (Artwork by David Bocquelet)

Originally developed for South Africa by Thomson-CSF and Matra, the R.440 Crotale was a fully automatic, all-weather, low-altitude SAM system. A Crotale battery consisted of two to three firing vehicles, each with its own fire-control radar and four ready-to-fire missiles (left), and a surveillance/acquisition vehicle equipped with the P4R search/target designation radar (older version is shown to the right). Portugal signed a Crotale purchase agreement in January 1974, in hopes of defending its more vulnerable African installations (including Bissau and Cabinda) from the growing threat of air attack. Portugal received a single Crotale battery in September 1974, after the war's end, and with Thomson's assistance it was resold to South Africa in 1976. (Artwork by David Bocquelet)

In early 1974 Portuguese authorities received reports that armoured vehicles intended for the PAIGC had been delivered to the Port of Conakry, raising fears of their imminent use in Guinea. Intelligence suggested amphibious BRDM-1 or -2 type armoured patrol vehicles, which were then in service throughout the Eastern Bloc. PAIGC forces first used these vehicles against Portuguese positions in Copá and Bedanda during January and March 1974, respectively. Their debut reportedly proved disastrous to the guerrillas, and the PAIGC's armour commander in Copá, Mamadú Cassamá, was killed during the fighting. (Artwork by David Bocquelet)

The Sud-Aviation (later Aérospatiale) SE.3160 Alouette III was the Portuguese Air Force's main helicopter in the war in Africa. Portugal acquired a total of 142 Alouette IIIs between 1963 until 1974, and the majority saw service in Angola, Guinea and Mozambique. The basic AL-IIIs performed transport, heli-assault, and medical evacuation operations, and were often joined by an armed variant equipped with a door-mounted 20mm cannon. Portugal explored the notion of arming its Alouette IIIs with 2.75 in. rocket launchers in 1973, but these experiments never reached the operational stage. This helicopter is painted in an olive-green paint that reduced infrared emissions, intended to mitigate the risks posed by heatseeking surface-to-air missiles. (Artwork by Luca Canossa)

On 6 April 1973 the PAIGC's anti-aircraft artillery group, under the command of Commandant Manuel dos Santos 'Manecas,' downed two Dornier Do-27s (3470 and 3333) with Strela missiles over northern Guinea. The first, piloted by Baltazar da Silva and carrying two passengers, crashed between Bigene and Guidage; there were no survivors. The second, piloted by António Ferreira with an army major, a wounded soldier, and a nurse on board, was shot down between Guidage and Bissalanca, killing all embarked. On the same day, a T-6 Texan taking part in the search for the missing planes was also shot down by a missile, killing the pilot. (Artwork by Tom Cooper)

The first Lockheed P2V-5 Neptunes, purchased second-hand from the Royal Netherlands Navy, began arriving in Portugal in April 1960 to replace the Lockheed PV-2 Harpoon. These maritime patrol aircraft were assigned to Air Base No. 6 (BA6) in Montijo, and several saw service as bombers in Africa, especially Guinea. In 1973-74 the Portuguese government petitioned the US to replace the ageing Neptune with the P-3 Orion, but the April Revolution delayed the order and, as a result, Portugal's P2V-5s remained in service until 1977. (Artwork by Paulo Alegria)

Portugal based a squadron of Fiat G.91 R-4 fighter-bombers in Guinea to support ground forces and conduct tactical reconnaissance. These jets were based at Bissalanca Air Base (BA12) and assigned to Esquadra 121. This unit was responsible for attack, fire support, and airborne command and control over Guinea, flying G.91s (the 'Tigres'), T-6s ('Roncos'), and Do-27s ('Cafeteiras'). At the end of March 1973, two G.91s (5413 and 5419) were shot down by Strela missiles fired by PAIGC guerrillas. During the first engagement, over the Guileje area on 25 March, the pilot managed to eject and was rescued; however, the second incident on 28 March, resulted in that pilot's death when his Fiat 5419 exploded in mid-air. (Artwork by Tom Cooper)

The Portuguese Air Force fielded two Fiat G.91 squadrons in Mozambique: Squadron 502 (the 'Jaguares'), at Aerodrome-Base No. 5 (AB5) in Nacala and Squadron 702 (the 'Escorpiões'), operating from Aerodrome-Base No. 7 (AB7) in Tete. FRELIMO forces were equipped with the Strela missile from 1974 onwards, forcing Portuguese pilots to be more cautious when planning missions. In 1974, Fiat 5433 took part in bombing missions against guerrilla bases during joint operations with Rhodesia over Tete province. Like the Fiat in Guinea, this G.91 also used a light bluish grey paint scheme. (Artwork by Tom Cooper)

The final year of the war in Guinea was the most challenging for Portuguese aviation, which lost six aircraft to Strela missiles. The impact of this new weapon on air activity was significant, but the Portuguese Air Force reacted swiftly and continued to fly combat operations over Guinea. Squadron 121's G.91s were critical in reacting to rebel initiatives, serving as the primary attack and tactical support platform for Portuguese forces in the closing months of the conflict. To reduce vulnerability to the heatseeking missile, G.91s in Guinea received an olive-green paint scheme expected to reduce the aircraft's infrared signature. (Artwork by Tom Cooper)

Despite an international arms embargo levied against it, in 1967 Rhodesia managed to buy a dozen Aermacchi AL-60B-2 light utility aircraft, which were assembled on site and given the local designation Trojan AL-60F-5. These aircraft were assigned to the 4th Squadron of the Rhodesian Air Force (RhAF) to carry out Forward Air Control (FAC) and Casualty Evacuation (Casevac) missions. In April 1974, the Rhodesians launched a joint operation with the Portuguese, Operation 'Marble,' in the Tete province of Mozambique. During this offensive against FRELIMO guerrillas, three Trojans were mobilised to support the Portuguese Brigade HQ at Estima Air Base, near the vital Cabora Bassa Dam. Rhodesia lost two Trojans during joint operations over Mozambican territory during 1974, both to Strela missiles: the first (R3244), piloted by Flight Lieutenant Chris Weinmann, on 14 April; and the second (R3427), piloted by Flight Lieutenant Willy Wilson and Flight Sergeant Roger Andrews, on 20 April. (Artwork by Luca Canossa)

The Percival Provost, the RhAF's basic training aircraft, was also conscripted for counter-insurgency operations. No. 6 Squadron at Thornhill flew a dozen Provost T.52s, which could be armed with two 7.62mm machine guns, four 5in. rockets or two 250lb. bombs. During the 1974 operations over Mozambique, the Provost was mainly used for search-and-rescue following the Trojan shootdowns, although these were critically vulnerable to Strela missiles themselves. It was not until sometime later that they were given a low-visibility infrared-reducing paint scheme. (Artwork by Tom Cooper)

In late 1962, the RhAF received a dozen ex-RAF Hunter FGA.9s for air defence and close air support duties. These jets were assigned to No. 1 Squadron at Thornhill Air Base, in Gwelo. During Operation 'Marble,' a joint offensive with Portuguese forces in April 1974, No. 1 Squadron's Hunters operated from bases in Rhodesia to attack targets in Mozambique. On the morning of 14 April, a pair of Hunters flown by Rick Culpan and Vic Wightman observed FRELIMO Strela missile fired while searching for a missing Trojan aircraft. Both aircraft escaped undamaged and that afternoon, four RhAF Hunters attacked a nearby FRELIMO base to discourage further missile attacks. The Hunters used 68mm Matra rockets in addition to 30mm cannons during these operations in Mozambique. These two examples are shown as after undergoing overhauls in South Africa of the early 1970s. (Artworks by Tom Cooper)

The Impala programme of the mid-1960s was extremely important for the development of the South African defence industry, which produced the small, Italian-designed jet trainer under licence. In SAAF service the MB-326 Impala Mk I was assigned to Nos. 4 and 5 Squadrons for advanced pilot training, and the single-seat Mk II light attack version followed the trainer into production. In 1969, the Pretoria regime expressed its willingness to lend some Impala Mk Is to the Portuguese Air Force for in-theatre pilot training at Luanda, but Lisbon declined. (Artwork by Luca Canossa)

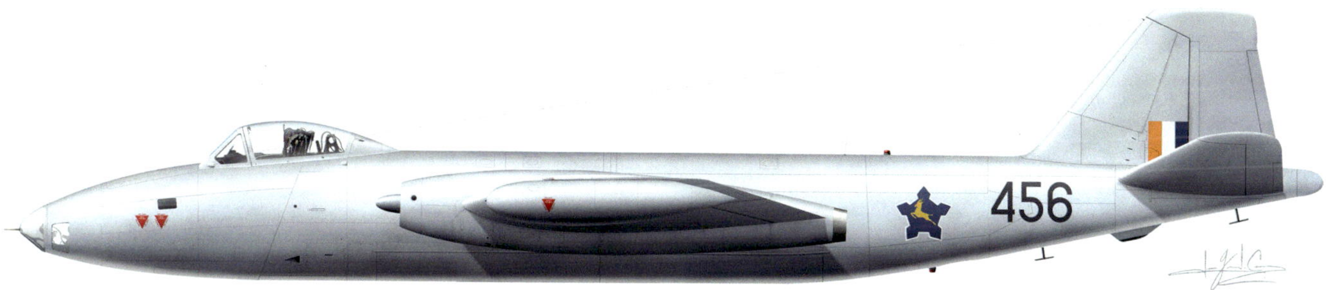

In 1962, the South African Air Force (SAAF) placed an order for six English Electric Canberra B(I).12s to fulfil requirements for a tactical bomber and high-altitude reconnaissance platform. The first Canberra arrived at Waterkloof Air Base in September 1963, and No. 12 Squadron became the SAAF's first jet bomber squadron. In 1974, South Africa deployed a Canberra to Luanda, at Portugal's request, for reconnaissance operations in northern Angola and Zaire. The Canberra arrived in Luanda a few days before 25 April, but flew no missions – the operation was cancelled soon after the change of regime in Lisbon due to the political sensitivity of South African aircraft operating in Portuguese territory. (Artwork by Luca Canossa)

The first Mirage IIICZ arrived in South Africa in April 1963, serving with No. 2 (Cheetah) Squadron at AFB Waterkloof, in south Pretoria. It was the first supersonic fighter in SAAF service. A few years later, in 1965, No. 2 Squadron received the Mirage IIIEZ, an improved version of its predecessor. In 1974, Lisbon, fearing Zairean intervention in Portuguese-held Angola, requested that SAAF Mirages perform 'intimidation flights' over the Angola-Zaire border and the vulnerable Cabinda enclave. A South African Mirage detachment was scheduled to arrive in Angola on 29 April and return to South Africa on 3 May, but the April Revolution in Portugal led to the cancellation of all planned SAAF missions from Angolan bases. (Artwork by Tom Cooper)

(Map by Tom Cooper)

Portuguese Marines in Mozambique. Unlike the regular troops, the special forces were well-trained and were feared by the guerrillas. (Ben Martin/Getty Images)

realised that the military command in Nampula already knew about this situation, but nothing had been done to contain it. In his contacts, he also realised that the settlers' revolt at the mess hall of the Beira officers, although initially spontaneous, had been instigated by a certain group of people and that the episode had been traumatic for the officers concerned, who were still perplexed by the fact that no measures had yet been taken to determine responsibility for what had happened.[11]

Costa Gomes prepared a report on the military situation in Mozambique, in which he noted that the war had worsened in several aspects, with the guerrillas trying to expand southwards, towards Beira and Vila Pery (Chimoio) and also towards the Zambezia region, in the centre of Mozambique. On the northern border, in Cabo Delgado, FRELIMO tried to entice the Macuas to extend subversion further inland and there were also guerrilla activities in Niassa, in the extreme north-west. Regarding the combat potential, Costa Gomes noted that at the end of 1973, there were 2,300 more men in Mozambique than at the end of 1972, but this reinforcement had been achieved at the cost of the retention of several units in Mozambique, delaying their redeployment to the following quarter. This situation could cause units to return to the mainland with a delay of three to six months. Even so, this reinforcement had allowed for an increase in the number of operations by about 10 percent, thus maintaining the operational exploitation.[12]

However, the relative combat potential was less favourable to the Portuguese forces, since FRELIMO had increased the number of guerrillas. Table 1 shows the numbers of the combatant units:

Table 1 – Relative combat potential

Effective	1972	1973
NT (a)	24,000	26,500
IN (b)	6,800	8,900
NT/IN RATIO	3.36NT/1IN	2.9NT/1IN

NT= Our Troops
IN = Enemy
(Source: RMM. HQ. 3rd Rep.)

If, in terms of men, the situation was more unfavourable to the Portuguese, in terms of equipment, the Portuguese troops also had several deficiencies. This included lack of military vehicles and firearms adequate to counter the guerrilla warfare, as was the case of 60mm and 81mm mortars, which the Portuguese troops needed. There was also a lack of training and preparation of the troops due to the lack of experienced officers and sergeants who were diverted to meet other needs. In addition there was also a lack of military strategy and coordination between civilian and military entities in the counter-subversion structures. It was therefore urgent to review the command structures, troop organisation and operations plans in order to gain efficiency in the fight against guerrilla warfare.[13]

One of the main measures that Costa Gomes defended was the transfer of the Headquarters of the Commander-in-Chief Chief from Nampula, in the north, to Beira, in the centre, with the creation of two sector commands (one in Beira and another in Vila Pery), given that the situation in central Mozambique was more dangerous than in the north of the territory.[14]The measure was defended in a personal letter he wrote to the Commander-in-Chief of Mozambique, on 20 February, in which he spoke of the measures that should be taken.[15] However, General Tomaz Machado did not agree, arguing that the transfer could be exploited psychologically by FRELIMO, besides being inconvenient due to the high financial costs and the changes in the communication system. The arguments put forward by Tomaz Machado partly convinced Costa Gomes, although CEMGFA considered that if the transfer of headquarters did not take place, a Central Military Zone should be created in the city of Beira, to coordinate all aspects of counter-subversion and counter-guerrilla in that area.[16] Costa Gomes was thus trying to find solutions in the military field, without questioning the political part, which was the real problem of the war.

The insistence on a military solution also led Portugal to take full advantage of the alliances it had with the white regimes in Rhodesia and South Africa to fight the guerrillas. Joint operations with these countries had been developed for several years and Rhodesia even used special forces and air assets in Mozambique to help the Portuguese (South Africa did the same in Angola). In the case of Rhodesia, this cooperation focused on the Tete area, which bordered Malawi, Zambia and Rhodesia and where the Rhodesian regime was facing the ZANU (Zimbabwe African National Union) guerrillas, who fought for the independence of Rhodesia. Since there was every interest in fighting both movements (FRELIMO and ZANU), Portugal looked to the neighbouring country for help in solving common problems.

It was in this context that Rhodesia deployed in April 1974, some air assets to the Estima airfield in Tete. The aim was to eliminate the columns of arms supplies coming from Zambia and passing through the Tete area.[17] The Rhodesians mobilised to Estima, four Alouette III helicopters armed with machine guns, two Percival Provost Mk 52 light aircraft and two Aermacchi AL-60F-5 Trojan planes armed with rockets. In addition, they also had on standby in Rhodesia, two English Electric Canberra bombers and four Hawker Hunter fighter-bombers. The Rhodesians also deployed a special force combat group to Estima.[18]

On 11 April, the Portuguese started collaborating with the Rhodesian military in reconnaissance and attack flights using the Trojan and the Canberra and on that very day, the Trojan was targeted by a Strela surface-to-air missile that had already reached the hands of the FRELIMO guerrillas.[19] This highly portable Soviet missile had already made its debut in Guinea with tragic consequences for the Portuguese Air Force (FAP) and was now arriving in Mozambique.[20] However, after what had happened in Guinea, the Portuguese Air Force in Mozambique was already prepared for the arrival of the missile and no plane was lost in the colony. The same fate did not befall the Rhodesians, who in the last weeks of April 1974, lost three planes in Mozambique hit by Strela missiles. These losses obviously made the Portuguese pilots uneasy, as they had to fly more carefully and follow a series of procedures to avoid missiles.[21]

Hoisting ceremony of the PAIGC flag on a detachment of the Revolutionary Armed Forces of the People (FARP), the armed wing of the PAIGC. These guerrillas were the most difficult that the Portuguese troops faced in Africa and the situation in Guinea did not cease to worry the political power in Portugal. (Albert Grandolini Collection)

In an interview with a South African journalist, the commander of the FAP in Mozambique, General Diogo Neto, complained that the political authorities did not allow Portuguese planes to bomb the FRELIMO bases in Tanzania. For Diogo Neto, it was important to have a retaliation strategy against the guerrillas, as well as a 'sophisticated intelligence network both inside Mozambique and outside the territory.' In the interview, the FAP commander also drew attention to the role of the civil administration in detecting enemy networks and that the native population should be concentrated in places controlled by the Portuguese, in order to create difficulties for FRELIMO in terms of support. Diogo Neto also urgently needed more and better aerial means to combat the guerrillas, although he considered that FRELIMO did not have the capacity to launch major attacks, only small attacks in isolated areas.[22]

However, subversion could spread over large areas of Mozambique and the role of the civil administration was important to prevent this. In short, the situation in Mozambique tended to worsen as FRELIMO carried out attacks in new areas of the territory, using increasingly sophisticated weapons such as Strela missiles. These concerns were present at the last meeting of the Mozambique Defence Council, on 11 April 1974. At that meeting, the situation in the colony was analysed and it was noted that in the northern provinces (Niassa and Cabo Delgado), the war had worsened. The guerrillas were also active in central Mozambique (Tete, Vila Pery and Beira). The Portuguese troops lacked resources and manpower, a situation that they tried to fill with local recruitment, although little was done in this area.[23]

Spínola obviously had a different view from Caetano on the resolution of the Guinea problem and tried to convince the leader of the government to negotiate with the PAIGC, but without success. (Revista do Povo Collection)

The problem of Guinea

Guinea was another territory where the military situation was very difficult. Located on the West African coast, the small colony was of little value to Portugal and in the global African context, it was the territory that should have had the least priority in the war effort; however, it was where the Portuguese forces faced the most capable guerrillas, with more firepower and manoeuvrability and with great material and political support. The PAIGC guerrillas had become a major problem for the Portuguese troops and the situation in Guinea was the one that generated the most concern in Lisbon.

Wreckage of a Portuguese Fiat G.91 (FAP 5419) shot down in southern Guinea by a Strela missile. The pilot could not eject and died. (Roel Coutinho Collection)

Marcello Caetano did not want to risk setting a precedent in Guinea by negotiating with the PAIGC, which was fighting for the colony's independence. For the head of the government, the case of Guinea could not be separated from the rest of Overseas Territories. This is what he explained to Spínola (who served as governor and commander of the Portuguese military forces in the territory from 1968 to mid-1973) in a letter at the end of February 1973:

> The case of Guinea has its particularities. But today it is part of a global problem of the country, it cannot be seen independently from the Portuguese overseas territory as a whole and there cannot be a policy for Guinea that is different from the one followed or planned for the whole overseas territory. Sometimes what would be very right for one part of the country cannot be done there, or at least must be postponed, because it would jeopardise the overall strategy.[24]

The wing of a Dornier Do.27 (FAP 3470) shot down in northern Guinea on 6 April 1973 using Strela missiles. None of the occupants of the plane survived. (Roel Coutinho Collection)

Spínola saw things differently and conveyed his displeasure to Caetano in a lengthy letter written a month later, in March 1973. In this letter, Spínola emphasized his anxiety about the war's extension, which could result in a military defeat for the Portuguese soldiers, as had happened in India. Caetano reaffirmed his refusal to negotiate with the guerrillas because they were determined to expel whites from Africa and drew the general's attention once more to the fact that any negotiations with the PAIGC would create a dangerous situation in the other colonies, where liberation movements would demand the same.

Shortly after this exchange of correspondence, Spínola had his most difficult time in Guinea. In late March, the guerrillas began using Soviet-made Strela surface-to-air missiles against Portuguese aircraft, managing to shoot down five planes in the space of two weeks. The first to fall were two Fiat G.91s jets and after wards were two piston-engined Dornier Do.27s and a T-6 Texan. The pilots were taken completely by surprise and did not even really understand what kind of weapon the PAIGC was using. The attacks were carried out in border areas, but the portability of the missile also allowed its gradual introduction into more inland areas of Guinea. Air power was the great advantage that the Portuguese forces had over the guerrillas and suddenly the FAP no longer had total freedom of action, which affected the morale of the Portuguese troops, who were used to having constant air support. In order to protect themselves from the missile, the pilots were forced to introduce a series of restrictions in their flight profiles, which made it difficult to provide air support to the ground forces, as well as to withdraw the wounded.

At the time, Otelo Saraiva de Carvalho was still in Guinea in the military command in Bissau and he says that the missile had a very negative impact on the morale of the troops, since 'the great supremacy of the Portuguese forces against the PAIGC really resided in the Air Force.'[25]

The importance of air power was also reflected in a letter that the commander of the Air Zone of Cape Verde and Guinea (ZACVG), Colonel Lemos Ferreira, wrote a few months later to General Costa Gomes. In this, he argued that the military survival of Guinea

PAIGC troops inside the Guileje barracks. The garrison was heavily bombedand the Portuguese troops eventually abandoned the position, which allowed the PAIGC to enter. (Albert Grandolini Collection)

relied almost exclusively on the personnel and means of the Air Force, given that the ground forces did not seem to be able 'to withstand and react to a strong shake for known reasons, namely their low motivation.'[26] The 'shake' to which Lemos Ferreira was referring had been the powerful attacks unleashed in May and June 1973, on the border garrisons of Guidage, Guileje and Gadamael.[27] In these attacks, the guerrillas had used a great concentration of means and personnel to bombard the garrisons over several weeks, using Strela missiles to protect themselves from the aviation. In Guidage and Gadamael, the Portuguese troops resisted the offensive, albeit with great difficulty but in Guileje, they abandoned the barracks, allowing the PAIGC to enter the unit. It was a great success for the guerrillas, who had never managed to conquer a Portuguese barrack.

For Spínola, it was the worst phase of the war, in which he even feared the collapse of the Portuguese forces. This is what he says in a letter dated 22 May and addressed to the Minister of Overseas Territories, Silva Cunha: 'We are getting closer and closer to the contingency of military collapse.'[28] In the same vein, he wrote to Costa Gomes asking for a reinforcement of means, no longer so much to obtain a military success, 'but only to prevent a collapse in the longer term.'[29]

In Lisbon, Spínola felt that the situation in Guinea was critical and that the military resources at his disposal were insufficient to face the new escalation of the war. In this way, he considered it essential to reinforce the means of intervention and armament in order to delay the collapse that was anticipated. The analysis made by the Commander-in-Chief of the Armed Forces in Guinea (CCFAG) was agreed with by the head of the CEMGFA office, Colonel Ramires de Oliveira, who on 28 May issued an opinion in which he 'considered the study of the situation carried out by the CCFAG to be clear, serene and frank, which subsequent events confirmed.' Ramires de Oliveira goes further in making political considerations about the war:

> (...) the national FA(Armed Forces), which have been fighting for 12 years in the Overseas Territories with deficient means, have not only contained the guerrillas but have also allowed the socio-economic and cultural development of the Portuguese space.
>
> The F.A. knew that its effort was necessary but that it was not enough and hoped that POLITICS would find possible solutions.
>
> At the end of this time, they are on the verge of facing an escalation in subversion which they are not expected to be able to tackle successfully.
>
> Examination of the strategic situation leads us to conclude that it is becoming necessary to review the political goals to be achieved in the knowledge that our military potential, with the means at its disposal, cannot fulfil the mission assigned to it up to now.[30]

On 6 June, Costa Gomes went to Guinea accompanied by Ramires de Oliveira, to better assess the situation. During his four days in the colony, Costa Gomes had the opportunity to talk with many of the military officers responsible for the conduct of the war. On 8 June, he presided over a high-level meeting at the headquarters of the Commander-in-Chief in Bissau with the officers responsible for the branches of the Portuguese forces in Guinea, as well as officers from the CCFAG's Staff. At that meeting, the head of the Information Department of the CCFAG, Lieutenant-Colonel Artur Baptista Beirão, made an overall analysis of the guerrilla forces, which had around 9,000 to 10,000 combatants, very well-armed, with great mobility and supported by foreign specialists – characteristics that gave them a great advantage over the Portuguese forces. The combat potential of the PAIGC allowed them to easily attack barracks in the border areas and even to annihilate those garrisons. In this officer's opinion, there was also a risk of an enemy air force intervening from Guinea-Conakry, since this country had some MiG fighter jets that could easily be used to attack any point in Guinean territory, leaving the main cities of Guinea, such as Bissau, Bafatá and Nova Lamego, at risk of an air threat.[31]

Brigadier Leitão Marques, who was the deputy operational commander of the CCFAG, agreed with this analysis and defended in that context, a retraction of the area garrisoned by the Portuguese to gain time and consolidate a final redoubt that, 'in extremis,' could guarantee a political solution to the war. The retreat of the Portuguese forces had to be done in a measured and phased way, retaining a series of key points, mainly the island of Bissau, associated with the regions of Bula and Mansoa, which should be maintained at all costs until the end. This retreat was aimed at preventing the annihilation of the border garrisons that were more vulnerable to PAIGC attacks and at reinforcing the Portuguese positions inside the territory by forcing the guerrillas to attack more deeply.

The remaining officers present agreed with the analysis of the situation and with the general concept of a withdrawal manoeuvre. However, the Air Force officer present, Colonel Moura Pinto, pointed out that regarding the possibility of intervention by enemy aerial means, the Portuguese forces were defenceless, having neither interception planes, nor anti-aircraft defence systems, nor radars that could counter such a threat. Spínola also agreed with the

PAIGC guerrillas in a moment of relaxation at a rear base in Senegal. From these bases they could easily attack Portuguese units near the border area and then retreat to sanctuaries in neighbouring countries. (Roel Coutinho Collection)

In mid-1973, Spínola eventually disagreed with Costa Gomes' proposed strategy of withdrawing units that were near the borders of Guinea. For Spínola, the native populations had over time, affirmed their loyalty to the Portuguese and could not be abandoned. The banner says: 'We also want to fight for a better Guinea.' (Revista do Povo Collection)

the PAIGC's growing combat capacity.

In view of the situation that had arisen, there was no other option but to leave the border areas for more rearward positions in the interior of the territory that would allow for a concentration of means. 'The growing strength of the enemy in the interior (…) requires us to pay special attention to the entire system and not only to the border garrisons, although these are a priority concern,' he said. Basically, it was an exchange of space for freedom of action, defended the general. This retreat would have consequences for the security of the populations that would be left to their fate, but this was a problem that had to be seen in the particular context of each ethnic group and that could be solved with the use of militias.

Costa Gomes also gave his backing to the outlined strategy, since, given the impossibility of significantly reinforcing the existing means, the only option was to reduce the occupied area and concentrate the garrisons in the interior of the territory. This would save forces and avoid the annihilation of the border garrisons, an event that would always have serious political and military repercussions.

It is interesting to note that la ended up changing his mind, when on 9 June, he wrote to the Minister of Overseas Territories, Silva Cunha, disagreeing, as governor, with the abandonment of the border areas and the respective populations that would be left without military protection; a measure he could not agree with, as he had personally committed to their security and socio-economic development. In this way, the withdrawal of the garrisons contradicted the commitments he had made to those populations, leaving him no choice but to abandon his duties in Guinea and return to the mainland.

At the end of July, Silva Cunha still went to Guinea to try to convince him to stay, but Spínola was not convinced, returning to Lisbon on holiday on 6 August and never returning to Bissau.[32] Just before Silva Cunha's trip to Guinea, Marcello Caetano had met in Lisbon with the ministers of Foreign Affairs, Defence, Overseas, Finance, and the Navy and with CEMGFA Costa Gomes, to analyse the situation in Guinea and take measures.[33] This important meeting took place on 1 August as part of the Higher Council of National Defence (CSDN) and the head of the executive analysed the situation in Guinea and what position the regime should take in the face of the worsening military situation. At the meeting, Caetano

Silva Cunha speaking in the ceremony in which Bettencourt Rodrigues assumed his new functions as military commander of Guinea. Right next to Bettencourt Rodrigues is Spínola. (António de Spínola Collection)

defended staying in Guinea and ruled out any possibility of negotiating with the PAIGC. For him, Portugal would lose a legal and moral weapon if it allowed any negotiations with the guerrillas. In his view, if the country went down this road, it would have to do the same in Angola and Mozambique, as well as having to negotiate the independence of Cape Verde, where there was no war.

The Minister of Defence, Viana Rebelo, suggested that a military study of the situation be carried out within 48 hours, but Caetano received the suggestion with reservations, as he was monitoring the situation on a day-to-day basis. Silva Cunha agreed with Marcello and recalled that he had always argued that there was no other solution but to fight for Guinea, without giving in on any point. For the Overseas Minister, the problem was one of 'global strategy,' particularly in the metropolis and if there were deficiencies, they had to be corrected. The Minister for Foreign Affairs, Rui Patrício, argued along the same lines, saying that the situation should not be exaggerated, but that there was little reason for optimism. Patrício argued that Portugal's military capabilities should be improved but he saw no other solution than to remain in Guinea. As far as can be seen from the content of the meeting, nobody, apart from Costa Gomes, admitted to the possibility of leaving the colony. In fact, the government's chief military adviser argued that if it was possible to defend Guinea, there was no other choice but to do so, but if it was not possible, the possibility of a withdrawal had to be considered. The general pointed out that after 12 years of war, the nation was tired and that the white population in the colony was even thinking of giving up. He emphasised that the most important thing was to avoid at all costs, a military defeat that would entail a political defeat.

Following the discussion, Caetano did not fail to respond to the CEMGFA, claiming that a military defeat did not always correspond to a political defeat, but that in the case of Guinea, an agreement with the PAIGC would be worse than a military defeat. In his view, a military defeat in which everything, except honour, was lost was preferable to negotiations with the enemy in which everything, including honour, was lost. Furthermore, if the problem was only Guinea, then the solution was simple and independence would be granted, but the capitulation of Angola and Mozambique would be catastrophic for the white population and the natives who supported the Portuguese cause. Therefore, he saw no other solution than to continue promoting the progressive autonomy of the Overseas Territories while maintaining the Portuguese presence in Africa, but if someone had a better answer to the problem, he would gladly give up his position [34].

Despite having no more detailed information about the rest of the meeting, it seems that Caetano asked Costa Gomes whether or not Guinea was defensible, to which the general replied that if the enemy did not show up for the war with their own aircrafts, Guinea was defensible. At the time, there was information from the Portuguese side that the PAIGC had a group of pilots receiving training in the Soviet Union and that the guerrillas could have Soviet aircraft in the near future.[35]

South African Defence Minister Pieter W. Botha in 1971 during a visit to London. Botha was a key player in helping Portugal. (UPI)

Costa Gomes also defended the redeployment of the Portuguese forces and the provision of more means to the Commander-in-Chief, but that the situation would be defensible if there was no further escalation of enemy means.[36] Given this assessment, Marcello Caetano decided that the Portuguese presence should continue and that everything should be done to provide the colony with an effective anti-aircraft defence.[37] It was also decided to nominate General Bettencourt Rodrigues to replace Spínola, an officer who had already been Army Minister (1968–70) and before that, Costa Gomes' assistant in Angola. According to Marcello Caetano, Guinea was in good hands.[38] As for reinforcements, two companies that were going to Angola (CCaç 4641 and CCav 8452) were diverted to reinforce the troops in Guinea.[39]

At the time, efforts were already underway to obtain a large loan from South Africa that would allow the purchase of most of the weapons Portugal needed to face the new stage of the war. Contacts in this direction had been on-going since July 1972, when in Mozambique, the Portuguese Defence Minister, Viana Rebelo, met his South African counterpart, Pieter Willem Botha. At this meeting, Viana Rebelo asked the South African minister for financial and material aid and following this contact, two lists of material were prepared: one of material to be provided by Pretoria and another of material to be obtained under a loan of 155 million rands (6.2 million contos).[40] This aid was to be used mainly in Angola and Mozambique, but with the worsening situation in Guinea, the Portuguese regime tried to obtain a larger loan.

On 29 May 1973, Botha passed through Lisbon on his way to Paris and had meetings with the Portuguese governors in which issues were discussed concerning the Alcora project and the material lists that Viana Rebelo had sent.[41]

At the end of August 1973, a team from the Ministry of Finance, led by the Secretary of State for the Treasury, went to Pretoria with the intention of requesting a loan of 250 million rands (10 million contos), but without any link to lists of equipment, although with a commitment to purchase equipment in South Africa whenever conditions were favourable in terms of quality and price.[42] The amount surprised the South Africans, who argued that it was too high for their means, but after several months of negotiations in Pretoria between the Portuguese ambassador in the country, Menezes Rosa and the Secretary-General of the South African Ministry of Foreign Affairs, Ambassador Bernardus Gerhardus Fourie, an agreement was reached at the end of the year. In this, the South African regime committed itself to a loan of 150 million rands (6 million contos), which would cover a large part of the Portuguese needs.[43]

Thus, minister Silva Cunha, who had only recently arrived at the Ministry of Defence (he assumed office on 7 November 1973) began to prepare an acquisition plan and received Botha a few days later to discuss various outstanding issues concerning cooperation with Pretoria.[44] However, the procurement plan for the armed forces would take time to materialise, while on the ground, the situation remained difficult. In Guinea, the PAIGC had declared the unilateral independence of the territory (24 September 1973), creating a new situation, which Portugal was trying hard to devalue.

The declaration of independence

The declaration of independence of Guinea-Bissau by the PAIGC, took place in a ceremony in the forests of Lugajole, east of Madina do Boé.[45] The PAIGC has prepared a big event for this ceremony with foreign guests and a military parade. The event was prepared in great secrecy to avoid any attack from the Portuguese forces and several journalists covered the ceremony which was reported in the international media.

A view of the PAIGC's popular national assembly, where independence was proclaimed on 24 September 1973. Besides the delegates, the PAIGC secretary-general, Aristides Pereira, can be seen speaking. (AFP)

The infantry of the new republic in 1973, on the day of the independence ceremony, with weapons supplied by eastern countries. (Bruna Amico Collection)

The declaration had an international impact, with dozens of countries recognising the existence of the new state and the United Nations (UN) General Assembly passing a resolution with 93 votes in favour, demanding the immediate withdrawal of Portuguese forces from Guinea-Bissau. In addition, on 19 November, Guinea-Bissau was admitted to the Organisation of African Unity (OAU), which could open the door to an intervention by African forces in the colony. On 26 November, Guinea-Bissau joined a United Nations agency for the first time: FAO – the UN food and agriculture agency – a sign that the PAIGC was infiltrating the UN through its specialised agencies.[46] The situation caused discomfort in Portuguese diplomacy, as it did not know what to do in international meetings where PAIGC delegates were also present.[47] Although the recognition of Guinea-Bissau's independence was far from unanimous, the truth was that the declaration of independence granted new support to the PAIGC and isolated Portugal more and more in the international context. Furthermore, it allowed the PAIGC and friendly countries to seek support for a possible candidacy of Guinea-Bissau for UN membership.

This can be seen in a letter that President Senghor of Senegal wrote to the Swedish Prime Minister Olof Palme, stating that Senegal was planning to present a proposal for Guinea-Bissau's membership in the UN General Assembly of September 1974. Senghor was seeking the support of Sweden and the Scandinavian countries to carry out this plan and sent the Senegalese Minister of Higher Education, Ouamane Câmara to Sweden, who accompanied the Senegalese ambassador to the country for talks on this issue.[48] On his return, minister Câmara wrote to Senghor informing him of the position of the governments of the Scandinavian countries, which could only recognise Guinea-Bissau as an independent country and admit it to the UN if the PAIGC controlled the entire territory of the colony, which was not the case. However, they were willing to continue supporting the struggle for independence and press Portugal to open talks with the PAIGC.[49]

Senegal also tried to pressure France to act with Portugal. On 19 February, the French ambassador in Dakar, Daufresne de la Chavalerie, had a meeting with the Senegalese Prime Minister, Abdou Diouf, with minister Ouamane Câmara also present. At that meeting, Abdou Diouf, recalled the results of Câmara's mission to the Nordic countries, hinting that these countries seemed determined to act in the direction desired by the Senegalese government, and that an approach by these countries to the Portuguese government would carry much more weight if France did the same on its side. Diouf also said that in a recent passage through Dakar, Dutch Foreign Minister Van Der Stoel – who was accompanying Queen Juliana on a visit to Ivory Coast – suggested to President Senghor that his government would be willing to recognise the independence of Guinea-Bissau, but that it could not take that position in isolation from the other countries of the European Economic Community.

However, the Dutch were available to make démarches with the other eight countries of the European community (France was also part of this group) so that a common public position could be taken, although the Dutch minister was convinced that France would not align with the other countries in a common position against Portugal. Hence Abdou Diouf's pressure on Paris to take a firmer position in relation to Portugal.[50]

Senegalese pressure did not convince the French and in an internal note from the Department of African and Malagasy Affairs (DAM) to the office of the Minister of Foreign Affairs, dated 4 March, those in charge of this section considered any joint or parallel démarche to pressure the Portuguese into negotiations in Guinea, to be counterproductive. For DAM, the Portuguese would react in the opposite direction to that desired by the European powers if they were to exert any kind of public pressure to force a negotiation. For this section, any meeting or contact should be bilateral and respect the traditional rules of secrecy and only in this way, could it have an effect on the Caetano regime.[51]

Since the PAIGC had declared independence, Portugal did everything in its power to devalue the declaration of Madina do Boé. In Guinea, the governor and military commander, Bettencourt Rodrigues, organised a visit by foreign journalists to Madina do Boé in November 1973, under heavy security measures. Of the three journalists accompanying Bettencourt Rodrigues, one worked for *Reuters* in Bonn, another for a German newspaper and the third for *Time* magazine. The delegation travelled by helicopter landing near Madina[52] and found that the area was uninhabited and there was no sign of the guerrillas. This led the journalists to conclude that the Portuguese forces control the region and that there were no liberated areas in which the government of the rebels exercised effective and permanent control. Bettencourt Rodrigues knew that the area was deserted, as he had ordered the Air Force to permanently reconnoitre the area and the planes had not detected any permanent guerrilla base.

For the new military commander of Guinea, the proclamation of independence had not had, for the time being, any effect on military operations. However, he considered that the appearance of a modern Air Force in the hands of the enemy, or of new missiles that would annul Portuguese aviation, could have serious consequences on the course of the war. He felt it was urgent to provide Guinea with modern anti-aircraft means based on surface-to-air missiles,[53] to reinforce the Air Force's attack and retaliation capabilities with new attack aircraft, which could retaliate in depth against neighbouring countries, and to have modern transport aviation (helicopters and light aircraft) that could provide mobility to ground troops.

After some military calm in late 1973, the guerrillas showed their strength again in early 1974, in eastern Guinea, with attacks on barracks and populations in border areas, namely Copá and Canquelifá. In mid-January, the Minister for Overseas Territories, Baltasar Rebelo de Sousa, visited Guinea, visiting several villages in the territory. The visit was organised with great care to get the message across that there are no liberated areas in Guinea and that Portuguese troops circulate throughout the colony. During his visits, Rebelo de Sousa also highlighted the progress that Guinea had experienced in recent years with various investments, taking advantage of the visit to inaugurate a beer and soft drinks factory whose investment (120 million escudos) was the largest investment made in the colony by private capital.[54] The minister did not limit himself to Bissau alone and went by helicopter to the south of the colony, visiting Cufar, Catió and Caboxanque, in the Cantanhez region, where the PAIGC was very active at the time.[55]

Meanwhile, in Copá, the Portuguese forces lost a Fiat G.91 at the end of January, which was providing support to that position, shot down by a Strela surface-to-air missile.[56] The small 52-man army detachment in Copá, made up of black and white soldiers, was even forced to abandon the position under pressure from the enemy. It was here that the PAIGC used armoured vehicles for the first time, in an attack on a Portuguese position, although without success.[57] Heavy shelling on 3 and 7 January was carried out by 120mm mortars and 122mm Grad-P rocket launchers, in addition to an armoured vehicle, which was used in the 7 January attack. The attacks were repelled by the Portuguese forces that were still in the detachment (27 men), but at the end of the month, the PAIGC

Overseas Minister Rebelo de Sousa during his visit to Guinea in 1974. Beside him, wearing dark glasses, is Bettencourt Rodrigues, the commander-in-chief of Guinea. (Horácio Caio Collection)

Another view of Rebelo de Sousa's visit to Guinea in 1974. These visits were well-organised by the regime to show the enthusiasm of the native populations and how much they liked the Portuguese. (Horácio Caio Collection)

attacked again and they shot down the Fiat G.91.[58] Despite being pursued, the pilot managed to elude the guerrillas and reach a Portuguese barracks on his own. He was then taken to Bissau, where he received an apotheosis.

However, it had been over six months since the guerrillas had shot down a Portuguese plane, a sign that the measures the Air Force had taken mid 1973 regarding the use of air power, had lessened the missile threat. Preparations were also underway to paint all the planes with a low-reflectivity dark green paint that would reduce the thermal signature of the aircrafts and thus diminish the missile's effectiveness. Another measure was the purchase in the USA, of an anti-missile system, launching thermal decoys that the Minister of Defence, Silva Cunha, had authorised in February 1974.[59] As for the helicopters, they would be equipped with a South African system, which deflected the hot air from the engine, whose purchase had also been authorised by Silva Cunha in March 1974.[60]

Also noteworthy, was the concern with the purchase of modern material for the Army, such as night vision devices for the G-3 rifles. This night vision equipment by intensified light would be used not only in the G-3, but also in heavy weapons and the acquisition would also imply binocular-type systems to be mounted on a tripod for ground observation. This type of equipment would have great advantages for the Portuguese troops since many guerrilla attacks took place at night. However, the purchase of these devices would drag on and the first ones only arrived in Portugal in October 1974, after the war had already ended and then only in small quantities.[61]

After the departure of the Portuguese from Copá, on 12 February, the PAIGC forces focused their attacks on Canquelifá, with the aim of driving back the Portuguese forces. The barracks were bombarded several times between January and March 1974, forcing the military command in Bissau to launch a retaliation operation in March 1974, with special forces – Operation Neve Gelada (Freezing Snow) – that dispersed the guerrillas in the area, causing several casualties.[62] This operation was carried out by the battalion of African commandos on 21 and 22 March and on the very first day, caused significant casualties to the guerrillas with 26 confirmed dead, including two Cubans and various captured war material. On the Portuguese side, there were two dead and 20 wounded.[63]

However, the shelling continued after this operation, with 120mm mortars, as Canquelifá was an obstacle to the guerrillas' progress in the north-east of Guinea. At the beginning of April, the company of hunters defending Canquelifá (CCaç 3545) was already in a highly worrying psychological situation and the Operational Grouping Command No. 2 (CAOP 2), in Nova Lamego, which was responsible for the area, called for the urgent replacement of the company and an immediate intervention by special forces for a long period, admitting that it also lacked the military capacity to deal with the situation. In the information received, there is also evidence of the guerrillas'use of ammunition with toxic gases, since the Portuguese troops in Canquelifá showed 'signs of intoxication caused by gases released and felt vomiting and nausea.'[64] The strong military pressure of the PAIGC on the area led Bettencourt Rodrigues himself to consider the abandonment of Canquelifá, as had already happened in Copá. In the opinion of the military commander of Guinea, both Canquelifá and Buruntuma (another border barracks) were difficult positions to defend and should therefore, be abandoned.[65]

The plan was to retract the military positions in the eastern zone, which had a high number of garrisons (around 150), in order to concentrate forces, thus increasing the capacity of the remaining garrisons to resist the guerrilla attacks and basically, to defend further inside the territory which made attacking the guerrillas easier, before they could retreat to the 'sanctuaries' they had in the neighbouring countries.[66] Besides the adjustments in the military garrisons which Bettencourt Rodrigues did not have time to make, there was a constant concern with the re-equipment of the Portuguese forces in Guinea, which were at a clear disadvantage against the guerrillas. In a note sent to Lisbon, on 20 April 1974, Bettencourt

A BRDM-2 wheeled armoured vehicle that the PAIGC received in the final phase of the war. (INEP)

of the BRDM-1 or BRDM-2 type in service in most of the Eastern Bloc armies.[68]

This information had also reached General Costa Gomes, who had already contacted the Spanish Army Chief of Staff, General Emílio Villaescusa Quilis, for the supply of anti-tank mines, with the latter committing to supplying 10,000 C3A anti-tank mines, produced in Spain.[69]

In March 1974, CCFAG made a presentation to Costa Gomes in which it concluded that the enemy had tactical initiative, forcing the Portuguese forces into a defensive attitude. There were several tactical advantages of the PAIGC forces, mainly due to the fact that they could move freely in neighbouring countries and had better military equipment and logistical support, which gave them a greater fighting capacity than the Portuguese. In turn, the Portuguese troops were too dispersed throughout the territory (226 garrisons), poorly led and instructed and the combat groups had an instantaneous firepower inferior to that of the enemy. There was a lack of artillery, tanks and anti-tank weapons, as well as a lack of effective anti-aircraft defence, capable of protecting the main urban centres and military units. Air resources needed to be reinforced in all types of aircraft and the reserves of the Commander-in-Chief only

Rodrigues expressed deep concern for the information he had about the use of armoured vehicles in a night attack in Bedanda (Cubucaré). Also about the consequences that the evolution of the combat potential of the PAIGC could have on the border garrisons, besides the strong limitations of intervention, especially on the issue of air.[67] The use of armoured vehicles by the PAIGC had worried the Portuguese forces for several months and there were reports that these vehicles had been landed in the port of Conakry in early 1974. The information indicated that they could be amphibious vehicles

The Alouette III was the main workhorse of Portuguese aviation in Guinea. Government plans foresaw the acquisition of more helicopters of this type in France. (Virgilio Teixeira Collection)

Portuguese Air Force CASA C-212-100-A-2P Aviocar on a trip to the Netherlands in the summer of 1979. This aircraft shows a low visibility anti-radiation paint to avoid missiles that would certainly have been used in Africa if the Aviocar had been employed in the war. However, this aircraft arrived after the war had ended. (Fred Willemsen Collection)

consisted of two battalions: African commandos and paratroopers, which limited the possibilities of manoeuvre.[70]

None of this was unknown in Lisbon, where Silva Cunha was now trying to re-equip the Portuguese forces with recourse to South African money. It was in this context that he continued negotiations with the French for the purchase of Crotale missiles and prepared the major acquisition, which would be the purchase of Mirage fighters. Besides these purchases, there was also the intention to acquire radars that allow good coverage of Guinean territory. He was also trying to equip the ground forces with more efficient weaponry, which would include the acquisition of rocket-propelled grenade launchers, some 155mm shells, as well as 120mm and 81mm mortars, which would allow a better response to guerrilla attacks. Some of these purchases for the Army would be made in Israel, after a visit made by a Portuguese delegation, in January 1974, to the Israeli defence industries.[71] Looking at the list of material, it can be seen that the major investments were destined for the Air Force.

The Secretary of State for Aeronautics, José Pereira do Nascimento, who was in charge of this dossier, had already called the attention several times to the need for new air means in Overseas Territories. In mid-1973, he recommended the purchase of 60 Alouette III helicopters, one SA 330 Puma helicopter, 30 Mirage fighters, 50 Skyvan or Aviocar transport planes, 120 Reims-Cessna FTB 337 (Milirole) planes and three mobile field radars.[72] In the final sum, the cost amounted to 5.5 billion escudos, which was almost the value of the loan granted by Pretoria. These plans were readjusted in 1974 in accordance with the value of the loan, the established needs and the number of light transport (Aviocar) and reconnaissance (Milirole) aircraft were reduced.[73] Without South African money, none of this would have been possible, which shows Portugal's dependence on this country to sustain the war.

Operation STOP

Meanwhile, in the South African capital, the main concern was the two southern colonies – Angola and Mozambique – which South Africa wanted to keep under Portuguese control. In Angola, the military situation was the least worrying at the end of 1973.

A UPA rebel at the start of the war in Angola in 1961. At the time, the rebels were still using simple weapons such as machetes and spears. However, they provoked several massacres between the white and black population in northern Angola, which led the Portuguese Army to react. (AP)

In northern Angola, the most active guerrilla movement was the National Front for the Liberation of Angola (FNLA), led by Holden Roberto, which had the support of Zaire and China. The FNLA had been at the origin of the armed insurrection in northern Angola in 1961, at that time called the UPA (Union of the Populations of Angola).[74] The UPA attacks marked the beginning of the war in

Luanda in the 1960s was one of the most prosperous cities in Africa and the population felt safe. At that time, war was a distant reality in the day-to-day life of Angolan cities. (José Matos Collection)

An MPLA training camp on the northern front in 1974, in the Republic of Congo, traditionally friendly to this nationalist movement, near the town of Dolisie and not far from the border with Cabinda. At the time, the MPLA was deeply divided between the Agostinho Neto and Daniel Chipenda factions. (José Luis de Pablos Collection)

Angola and led Salazar to send troops to the areas affected by the rebellion, who expelled the UPA elements. Since then, the FNLA guerrillas had not been able to expand their area of operation to the north, nor to obtain significant results.

The Popular Movement for the Liberation of Angola (MPLA) in eastern Angola was no better. It had withdrawn to Zambia and was only sporadically active along the border. At the time, the MPLA was suffering from strong internal tensions, with two factions attacking each other, one led by Agostinho Neto and the other by Daniel Chipenda. There was also the National Union for the Total Independence of Angola (UNITA), led by Jonas Savimbi, who was trying to attract the dissident faction of Chipenda's MPLA and who had the support of China, which simultaneously, supported UNITA and the FNLA, in the hope that one of the two movements would fill the vacuum left by the MPLA which at that point, had no strength or cohesion.[75] In short, the military situation in Angola was under control mainly due to the lack of unity among the guerrilla groups, who did not understand each other. For many of the residents of the colony, the war was a distant reality that was not felt in the cities, where most of the population lived. Luanda was a prosperous city, as were other cities scattered throughout the territory and a large part of the population felt safe, not fearing the guerrillas.

However, by early 1974, the military command in Luanda began to fear a major attack on the enclave of Cabinda by FNLA forces, supported directly or indirectly by Zaire. Cabinda represented a particular problem in the Angolan context because it was isolated

A South African Canberra B (I) 12 in flight. In April 1974, one of these bombers was stationed in Luanda for reconnaissance flights in northern Angola. (BAE Systems)

Another aircraft that was due to be used in Angola was the South African Mirage IIIEZ. However, the deployment never took place. (Daan Conradie Collection)

from the rest of the colony and was a small territory that could be easily conquered by force. To contain this offensive, General Luz Cunha, who commanded the military forces in Angola, decided to reinforce the combat resources he had in Cabinda to anticipate any enemy action.[76] The reinforcement would be phased in but would eventually take the form of sending two companies, two batteries of field artillery and one anti-aircraft battery, as well as support from the Air Force, consisting of two B-26 bombers, a DO-27 light plane and an Alouette III helicopter armed with cannon. In this context, it was also decided to authorise fire actions by aviation in reaction to possible enemy attacks, namely in the People's Republic of the Congo, whose territory bordered Cabinda and Zaire. In addition, orders were given to carry out aerial reconnaissance over Congolese

An Impala Mk 1 of No. 5 Squadron of the South African Air Force (SAAF) near AFB Pietersburg during a low-level navigational exercise. Pretoria even offered the Portuguese the possibility of training in the Impala Mk 1, but the offer was refused. (Herman Potgieter Collection)

territory to detect possible guerrilla bases, which could then be attacked by special forces.[77]

The reconnaissance missions were to be undertaken by a South African Canberra bomber that would be deployed to Luanda to conduct these operations. The South African involvement had been decided at a high-level meeting in Cape Town on 21 February 1974 between the Angolan Commander-in-Chief, General Luz Cunha and Admiral Beermann of South Africa, and had been approved by South African Defence Minister P.W. Botha.

Botha later wrote to Silva Cunha offering to deploy South African air assets to Angola, namely Mirage III fighters and Canberra bombers.[78] The Mirages were to be used to conduct intimidation flights along Angola's northern border, while the Canberra was to conduct photographic reconnaissance flights along that border, including over the Cabinda enclave and also over the Congo and Zaire, in order to monitor the guerrilla bases. The Mirage was scheduled to arrive in Luanda on 29 April, then travel to Cabinda and return to South Africa on 3 May[79]. The Canberra arrived in Luanda a few days before 25 April but never left the Angolan capital. With the change of regime in Lisbon, the whole operation would be cancelled due to the presence of South African aircrafts in Angola that was considered inconvenient.

It was not the first time that the South Africans provided aircraft to support the Portuguese in Angola. In 1969, the Pretoria regime had already expressed its willingness to lend some Aermacchi MB-326 (Impala Mk 1) training planes to train pilots in Luanda, but Portugal refused.[80] The only aircraft loaned by the South Africans and accepted were the old T-6 Harvard, which Portugal used in Africa until the end of the war.[81]

4
THE BIRTH OF THE MFA

In February 1974, the captains' movement already had a sizeable organisation with a vast network of contacts extending to the African territories. It did not yet have a defined political programme, but some of its members cherished the idea of overthrowing the regime through a military coup. As for the political programme, it began to be defined at a meeting near Lisbon, in Cascais, on 5 March.

However, despite these movements, the regime was officially, far from knowing what was going on in the captains' movement, as can be seen in the 'Periodic report of counter-subversion' in the metropolis, referring to the month of February 1974, prepared at the level of the Army General Staff. On green sheets of paper and with a red stamp reading 'confidential,' the Deputy Chief of Staff of the Army, Fernando Viotti de Carvalho, presented the situation in the mainland.

As a result of the survey carried out by the Army General Staff (it is not stated how the data was obtained or by whom), during that period 'there was no evidence of substantial changes in the mood of the civilian populations. However, the generalised state of concern continued in the face of the significant increase in the cost of living that has been triggered since the end of last year as a result of the so-called 'energy question.' As negative factors, the report pointed out the economic situations of the militia corporals and soldiers, the deficient medical assistance and the insufficient funds allocated to the messes.

The Army characterised the state of the country in the second month of 1974 'by a strong effort of the subversive movements in the sense of mobilising the masses for the realisation of street protests which, despite being profusely encouraged through pamphlets and mural inscriptions, did not obtain significant expression.' At the same time, it reported that, 'reflexively,' there had been 'an increase in the diffusion of propaganda aimed at the military, as can be seen from the detection of leaflets and mural inscriptions that took place in units and in their surroundings.' The document, signed by Viotti de Carvalho, informs that several incidents were registered in canteens because the food was allegedly not in good condition; there were initiatives in universities; flyers with the indication 'People's war on the colonial war' were found in Braga and other subversive slogans relating to the war in Overseas in Coimbra; a cardboard box containing an unexploded petard and subversive propaganda flyers was found, as well as flyers in Figueira da Foz with the inscription: 'Boycott the classes – 21 February – 13 years of colonial war, enough is enough.'

Still in the military, on 4 February, cards with contents considered subversive and subscribed by 'anti-colonialist military' were detected in Lisbon. In Viseu, pamphlets were found alluding to 4 February – date that marks the 'beginning of terrorism in Angola' and in Coimbra, the cards urged the soldiers to 'fight against the colonial war.'

From 12 to 21 February, leaflets had been spread by the 'anti-colonial Popular Resistance propagating street protests for 21 February – in the vicinity of the units of the Heavy Artillery Regiment 3 (RAP 3) of Figueira da Foz, the Infantry Regiment 1 (RI 1) of Lisbon; Infantry Regiment 5 (RI 5) of Caldas da Rainha; the Practical School of Military Administration (EPAM) in Lisbon and in HMR 1 of Porto.'

The Army had already called attention to the existence of five dates considered 'sensitive' for the months of April and May: 14 April – Angolan Youth Day; 17 April (in 1969 it was the day that marked the beginning of the academic crisis, when students were not allowed to speak at the inauguration of the mathematics building in Coimbra); 22 April – Lenin's Day; 24 April – day of struggle against colonialism and for peaceful coexistence; and 1 May – Workers' Day. The military that would launch the coup d'état, would precisely choose the week of 20 and 29 April to carry out their action, avoiding 1 May and the following days, as this was a time when the regime would be more vigilant to street movements.

However, the report concluded that, despite the occurrence of two disorderly demonstrations in Lisbon, a general climate of public order and tranquillity was maintained in the metropolis. Despite this conclusion, the document still mentions the existence of some factors that affect the state of mind in the military environment, without specifying which ones. Also in the same report, in an annex, information considered to be of direct interest to the Armed Forces is given on the topic 'Self-determination of the Overseas Provinces and the Immediate End of the War.' During the period under review, no 'innovations of substance or form' were noted in the treatment of this theme.

On the sub-theme of 'subversion of the Armed Forces,' the radio-communist propaganda aimed at subversion within the Armed Forces, in particular, did not show any 'special features' in relation to what was recorded in the previous report. However, there were again 'alluded to circulations' of subversive leaflets and posters in military units.[1] The report is completely silent on the release of Spínola's book, as well as on the conspiratorial movement within the Armed Forces. As for the months of March and April, if there were reports of this kind, they are not in the archives.

It is interesting to note that although the report was written at the level of the Army leadership, the latter seemed to be completely unaware of what was happening within the military institution. The same was true for PIDE/DGS, which was taken by surprise by the April coup.

Stage performance at the National Assembly

The President of the Council entered the month of March in an environment of disintegration that was beginning to grow on several fronts and felt the need to maintain the appearance that the regime was secure. The waves caused by the position defended in Spínola's book and endorsed by the CEMGFA, proposing a political solution for the war, in confrontation with the positions taken by the government of maintaining the war in Overseas Territories, spread, and were felt within the Army in Portugal and in the colonies.

It was a very delicate situation (in the words of the head of government himself), already entrenched between the President of the Republic, the two generals and the movement of captains that these two apparently controlled. The depth of the crisis is illustrated in some private correspondence from the Head of Government during this period: on March 1 Caetano receives a letter signed by Francisco Vale Guimarães, civil governor of Aveiro, who states that Spínola's book is generating 'serious disturbance.' Vale Guimarães says that one has to admit that even among 'the people' linked to the regime there are those who prefer the theses of the general to those of the government, even on 16 [February] 'so magnificently expounded by your Excellency' (referring to the speech at the close of the annual conference of ANP – Popular National Action). The publication of the book, at such a complex moment, was 'a disservice, with the aggravating factor of the general having an impact on public opinion. More than ever, it is important to close ranks, in force, around your Excellency.'[2]

About a month earlier, on 3 February, Caetano received another similar letter from Mário Bacelar Begonha, nautical officer and professor at the Military Academy, who reported 'the great confusion in the minds of some Portuguese who are actually less enlightened or trustful in the head of the government.' For this officer, 'the President of the Council' is aware of all the 'manoeuvres' and 'coups' and will not allow himself to be intimidated either by any 'pronouncement' or even by 'any publication' that intends to lead to the so-called 'palace revolution.' Mário Begonha even says that what he finds most difficult:

> (…) at the present moment is not to lose serenity or determination. In fact, when one believes in a cause, in an idea and in a person, it does not seem that any 'alarm' or startle is justified and even less so that people start to doubt the capacity and value of that leader in whom they believed until very recently.[3]

Since the President of the Republic did not accept his resignation from the government, Marcello Caetano did not have the courage to 'slam the door' either, because 'psychologically he is not capable of abandoning those who had invited him to the position.'[4] He decided on an act designed to answer the generals and clarify public opinion.

Caetano used what he called 'constitutional legality' and proposed to the Overseas Committee in the National Assembly that it study a motion to present to the parliament so that no doubts remained about the country's overseas policy. The aim was to submit the text of the motion to the National Assembly for ratification.

The head of government chose to side with the most conservative positions of the regime by making an uncompromising defence of Overseas Territories in a speech to the National Assembly. The speech was scheduled for 5 March, a day that would go down in the history of the captains' movement.

General Andrade e Silva, who in 1973 became Minister of the Army. (National Defence Archive)

Caetano's expectation that he might announce the dismissal of the two generals, due to the publication of the book, the captains reaffirmed to Spínola the support of the movement.[6]

On 4 March, the political state of the country was mirrored: Caetano rewrote old speeches to justify keeping the war in the face of the position of the two generals and a one-party National Assembly; the first debate/discussion on the impact of the book was held at the Army Ministry with the participation of commanders from various military regions of the country; and the captains' movement prepared the drafting of a political manifesto calling for an end to the war, regime change and the democratisation of the country.

Within the regime, there was a bloc made up of the Government and the Presidency of the Republic, which tried to resist in a veneer of power and with no other solution than to close ranks around the old buzzwords (as will be seen in Caetano's speech).

Of the discussion in the Army Ministry on 4 March, only a small note, distributed without any explanation by the daily press, radio and television, would emerge for public opinion. The government only informed that 'a working session' had been held that morning in the Army Minister General Andrade e Silva's office, attended by the Minister and the Under-Secretary of State, Viana de Lemos, the Generals Chief of Staff of the Army, Deputy Chief, Quartermaster General, Assistant General, Director of the Institute of Advanced Military Studies, and Commanders of the military regions of Lisbon, Oporto, Coimbra, Tomar and Évora. As to the content, nothing transpired for the public.[7]

However, and according to the records of the meeting, the concerns with the impact of Spínola's book were causing great apprehension, evident in the topics to be discussed: 'history of the book, written by someone who had been governor of Guinea and published after being named Vice-CEMGFA, he asked for permission to publish the book, and it was given the attached information from the head of the EMGFA (Costa Gomes) and the order from the Minister of National Defence.' The Army Minister began the meeting by stating that the Government's overseas policy was well defined in the Constitution and in Caetano's speech at the ANP annual conference, held last 16 February. He cited articles of the Constitution, the statutes of Angola and Guinea and the most significant passages of the Prime Minister's speech.

Having passed this point, the next problem to be focused on was '*Portugal e o Futuro*,' although the meeting was not intended to discuss the solution presented (by Spínola, i.e., the political path to war) but rather for each person to 'meditate' on what corresponded to a policy contrary to that expressed in the Constitution and to that followed by the Government, everything else was secondary.

The participants in the meeting learnt that the scope of the book had gone beyond the Army Ministry, but what mattered at that

In fact, the movement continued to conspire and on 2 March, a meeting to join forces between the cadet officers' commission and the militia officers' commission was held at the home of Major Vítor Alves, one of the military officers most active in coordinating the movement. Captain Armando Marques Ramos was appointed liaison between the two commissions. The Air Force commission met, according to Otelo, to 'put the finishing touches on its definitive document.'

During the meeting, Major Hugo dos Santos proposed: 'We know that you don't want to ally with us until your problem is solved. We wanted to make you a proposal to work together: first you overthrow the regime and then we give you our word that your problem will be solved.' From that moment on, the two movements decided to work together. The union of the two allowed the meeting in Cascais three days later.

The Drafting Committee for the Army's programme-document was to meet in Miraflores, Algés, at the home of Captain Pilot Seabra with the Air Force committee and others from the Navy. It had the purpose of drawing up the definitive version of the final manifesto of the 'Movement of Armed Forces Officers' called 'The Movement, the Armed Forces and the Nation,' to be presented two days later in a plenary session. Representatives of the three branches of the Armed Forces were present. The Navy representatives stated that they would only bind themselves to a progressive political programme, accepting to be in Cascais as observers. The representatives of the Air Force expressed their disagreement with the solution advocated for the colonial problem and stated that they would be present at the Cascais meeting to affirm this.[5]

On 4 March, the movement's Coordinating Committee met again to prepare the following day's plenary session. Before entering the meeting's agenda and given that Marcello Caetano was to give a speech the following day at the National Assembly, they decided to send Vasco Lourenço and Otelo Saraiva de Carvalho to a meeting at António Spínola's residence, to try to obtain information about the meaning of the President's communication. Faced with moment was that 'it could exert an extraordinary influence' on the psychological state of the soldiers in combat – direct influence – and also on their families – indirect influence, and on the general population of the metropolitan and Overseas Territories. There was also the concern with international opinion, in particular that which would invariably boost the morale of the movements considered to be terrorist by the regime. The commanders of the military regions were recommended to be firm with the unit commands, as the Government was worried about possible harmful influences at that level.

Once the guidelines had been exposed, a period of dialogue was opened, in which the Chief of Staff of the Army (CEME) began by assuming 'the aspect' that a clandestine organisation had developed in the Army, which 'certain measures had practically deactivated,' but he feared that the appearance of the book would revive its action. He was obviously referring to the captains' movement, which he thought had been deactivated.

The records of the meeting are clear:

> The book would allow the opening of a split within the Armed Forces and especially within the Army; it would affect the Army's morale, both of the combatants and their families; it would allow external pressures to be exerted on the combatant troops; it would allow one to have an image, not necessarily correct, of the national situation and of the difficulties at the enemy's level. In his contacts with civilian elements, he noted that there was enormous confusion in people's minds.

The CEME concluded that the situation could result in a weakening and disciplinary problems that had to be avoided, and once the military apparatus was weakened, the Government's freedom to pursue the policy under way would be reduced. In his speech, the commander of the Oporto military region said that he had already started clarification visits to his units. However, he considered that there was a problem to be solved: explaining to the population.

The commander of the Tomar military region also intervened in the same vein and expressed his doubts because the author of the book was second in rank in the Armed Forces. In addition to this position, the director of the Institute of Advanced Military Studies pointed out that Spínola was the most decorated operational commander who had stated that military action was unviable due to the lack of human resources,

The commander of the Coimbra military region took note of the firm position taken, but feared that without other actions, thesituation would become difficult to maintain, as the split already existed, there being officers who took the book as a bible and that of the two parties that could be formed, victory would fall to those who spoke out and had superior support.

The command of the Oporto Military Region considered that the situation was serious because if a movement was outlined it would have a 'head.' The Governor of the Lisbon region questioned those present about whether, if Spínola did not perform those functions, the book would not be considered a subversive document. He had no doubts about the firmness directive, but he considered indispensable, the existence of a written document to support the regional commanders and that a clarification to the population was necessary.[8]

The answer was to be found in the speech that the Head of Government would make the following day in the National Assembly and which was also destined to be published in newspapers and broadcast on the radio. However, the opinions expressed at the meeting showed the dominant thinking in the military top brass: the Overseas Territories were to be defended and the war was to continue.

However, if in Portugal, the information published was controlled by the political power through prior examination (the name given to censorship exercised on the press by the regime), the same was not true in other countries, as can be seen in the correspondence sent to the President of the Council by the diplomatic and consular representations, which sent Marcello Caetano that which was being published in the foreign press.

On 26 February, the Portuguese embassy in London reported the echoes of *Portugal e o Futuro* in the press, saying that articles had appeared in the *Guardian* newspaper, in the Finnish newspaper *Rhodesia Herald* (27 February), in the *London Times* (2 March) and there were even Danish newspapers that headlined (4 March) 'famous general bows down to African realities.' Nearer to that, in Madrid, it was published (4 March) in the magazine *Triunfo*, which for the 'first time from within the regime opinions were being expressed which when they were uttered by the opposition were severely punished.' The Spanish newspaper *Informaciones* highlighted in its headline: 'A military victory overseas is not possible.' According to the embassy in Rome, Italian newspapers considered the situation in Portugal critical due to the appearance of the book.

From Paris, on 13 March, the embassy highlighted the title of *Figaro*: 'Agitations in the FA – the book of a general revealing a deep crisis.' The correspondence dealing with references to *Portugal e o Futuro* in telegrams from Portuguese diplomatic and consular representations abroad, occupies three files in Marcello Caetano's archives.

Caetano began his speech to the National Assembly on 5 March by stating that 'there can be no doubt that the most serious problem currently facing the Nation is overseas,' showing that he knew that the country's main problem was overseas and the colonial war.[9]

For the President of the Council, the country and the evolution of the 'pluricontinental and multiracial' society was being disrupted by growing international pressure:

> A pressure that finds in the constitutional or dependent assemblies of the United Nations the favourable environment for formation, amplification and application. And from which flows the most incredible campaign against our country (…) and with the use of the most varied weapons from slander to aggression. In the face of this attack, which everything indicates is on the increase, the Portuguese people must adopt a conscious and defined attitude. And so, we ask you, through your highest representative assembly, to reflect.

In this sense, it decided to 'recapitulate' the orientation that had been followed by the Government, 'within the lines traced in the constitutional revision of 1971.' The struggle of more than a decade in the Overseas Territories was justified by the fact that one cannot 'fail to protect populations whose will is to remain Portuguese, nor to preserve a work of civilisation erected and maintained by the work and grace of Portugal and which will only subsist with Portugal.' In an indirect provocation to Spínola's book, he asked:

> Have we been wrong? In Africa we are not only defending whites, but all those who, regardless of their colour (…) are loyal to Portugal and for this very reason, in case of abandonment, would be victims of enemy revenge. On the other hand, there is

a global defence of the Overseas Territories that requires us to be consistent in our attitudes. A compromise or abdication in one place would immediately affect the strength of the resistance as a whole [response to the impossibility of the negotiating path Spínola wanted]. We could not, for example, accept negotiations with the enemy in Guinea on terms that would deprive us of the authority to refuse negotiations in Angola or Mozambique. Therefore, only the central government can have the initiative – because it has the responsibility – to conduct overseas policy. Only the government together with the other sovereign political bodies – and not any other entities.

This was the end of his reply to Spínola, repeating arguments that he had already used before in letters exchanged with the general, but the speech was still without novelty, since this elocution was based on others uttered previously.

On the future, he said it is:

(...) a road that takes some time to travel (...). We need time. We need to buy time if we want to proceed honestly. Would it be possible to accelerate political solutions? This is where a frank and open debate can take place. We have already provoked it in the country on the occasion of the 1969 elections and the response of the electorate was categorical. This debate cannot be permanently admitted for reasons that have been set out more than once. First, because according to the general consensus, the preparation of a decision can be discussed. But when the decision has been taken, and especially if that decision is so serious for national life, that it demands the mobilisation of minds, the sacrifice of resources and attentive and risky military service, it is not licit to discuss every day afterwards the decision that is executed and the execution of what has been decided. Secondly, because the country is engaged in a fight with powerful enemies who have no lack of means of psychological pressure or money to flood us with their propaganda, this debate would be a breach provided to the enemy to spread their lies with more shamelessness than they already have.

'In the five years and five months that I have been responsible for the government of the country, not a single day has passed in which the overseas problems have ceased to be present in my mind,' he said, alluding afterwards to the soldiers and the populations who were in the colonies: 'There is a responsibility that I do not want for myself: that of abandoning them.'

At the end, pretending to give power back to the members of parliament to decide whether or not to maintain the path he had set out, he concluded:

The Government over which I preside has committed itself to a course of action. And it cannot renege on its commitments. But neither I nor any of the men who are with me in the government, none of us occupy our posts out of personal ambition. We are motivated solely by the spirit of serving the national interest, the spirit of serving our common Homeland in the best way possible. It is now up to the National Assembly to say whether the course we are following is the right one' [promising that he would submit to its verdict].[10]

In his memoirs, Otelo Saraiva de Carvalho recalls the repudiation the speech provoked in him, as in his opinion, it was nothing but a fraud. 'As if Marcello did not know that it was exactly what the Assembly wanted to hear and then, standing up, give a warm applause, in an acclamation already decided beforehand.'[11] It is curious to note in this regard that the Minister of the Navy, Pereira Crespo, recounts in his memoirs that Costa Gomes appreciated Marcello's speech, as if he agreed with it.[12]

After the President of the Council's speech, the pro-Ultramar motion of the Overseas Commission was presented by its president, Neto de Miranda, which was under parliamentary discussion until the 8th, when the renewal of the overseas policy would be approved.

The government services sent Caetano's speech and the motion to ratify the overseas policy, to the newspapers, which reproduced them for several days, reporting the 'unanimity' of the National Assembly. Caetano himself sent a copy of his speech to his Spanish friend Laureano López Rodo, professor of Administrative Law at the University of Madrid, Minister of Planning and Economic and Social Development and Minister of Foreign Affairs in Spain.

If, in his speech, Marcello Caetano seemed to give the National Assembly the final word on what the country's overseas policy should be, what he wrote later, showed how parliament only served to be used in his quest for the legitimisation of power, which was increasingly at stake.

Caetano said in his memoirs, that a three-day debate took place during which 'the usual oratory gushed out, in which the lack of political preparation of most of the deputies was once again manifested.'[13] The former head of government here reveals a contradiction which reinforces the thesis of staging: if the MPs were unprepared, then why consult them and ask them to ratify the main policy of his government? Or was the President of the Council isolated, with no other way of legitimising himself?

Marcello did not appreciate that some of the speakers wanted the motion to emphasise the desire to speed up the autonomy of the overseas provinces. One of them (Mota Amaral), the youngest deputy, coming from the previous legislature where he was in the ranks of the liberals, placed particular emphasis on this thesis, being consistent with what he had already defended in the past, that is, that the colonies should have progressive autonomy and it should not only be administrative but also political in terms of legislation and government.[14] Although he was not an advocate of the independence of the colonies, Mota Amaral thought that they should have greater political autonomy.

In addition to the divisions that arose among members of parliament, the President of the Council's initiative to address the National Assembly was also criticised by the Head of State. Américo Thomaz noted that he had no prior knowledge of the communication and questioned why the parliament had been consulted. Thomaz argued that the 'cover' requested from the National Assembly signified the existence of 'inadmissible' doubts and was yet another sign of 'dangerous indecisions and weaknesses, no less serious in the existing situation.'[15]

Still on the role of the National Assembly, the deputy editor of *Diário Ilustrado*, Jorge Tavares Rodrigues, wrote to the President of the Council on 22 February 1974. Addressing the President and his friend after the presentation of the magazine *A Semana*, published in Paris for emigrants scattered throughout Europe, he stated that he had heard several people and that:

One of the most important problems to be faced will be the weakness of the National Assembly – weakness that now would matter so much if it did not exist since it would be its duty to issue an opinion that the nation would respect. But it does not. Let us not deceive ourselves! The country forms an image of the Assembly which is not far removed from the sad reality it portrays. It is a reality that even justifies apprehensions in terms of loyalty. (...) yesterday in the Assembly [there were] some who openly criticised your 'demagogy' and the insufficient manner in which you responded to General [Spínola].

Jorge Tavares Rodrigues alerted Caetano to the fact that the youth did not consider the Overseas Territory, nor know it as a parcel, of their territory and on Spínola he predicted: 'There are those who believe that the general's resignation is the inevitable consequence and remedy ... for some time. Others are confident that the Armed Forces and many civilians easily won over by the general's doctrine will take positions adverse to the government and that there will not cease to be disturbance of public order.'[16]

On the other hand, in agreement with the content of the speech, Álvaro Roquete, director of the Directorate-General of Tourism, also referred in a letter to Caetano what he considered to have been the extraordinary speech in the National Assembly. He felt it to be opportune, fair and serious, noting the judicious path taken by the head of the government but unfortunately noting that the book that gave rise to the speech, caused so many divisions among the Portuguese. He warned that any compromise by the government at this time would be extremely serious.[17]

It is interesting to note that Caetano himself was also convinced of the wide repercussion of the speech, as he pointed out that after the 5th of March, he received countless letters in the Presidency of the Council, many of them praising him.[18] While Caetano took pleasure in the letters he received; the captains' movement gained political consistency.

MFA clarifies positions

The decisive meeting for the birth of the MFA – *Movimento das Forças Armadas* – took place on 5 March, in Cascais, with the presence of 194 officers from the three branches of the Armed Forces, although the Army was the most represented. At this meeting, a document entitled 'The Movement, the Armed Forces and the Nation' was presented, which drew attention to the impossibility of winning the war and that the Armed Forces could be held responsible for a military failure. This solution had to consider the interests of the Portuguese in Africa, but also the interests of the African peoples who aspired to their own government. The military members of the movement knew that the political power in force would not allow such a solution and that, in this case, it would be necessary to democratise the regime in order to solve the serious problems that Portugal was facing. The document obviously generated controversy among those presents and the Air Force and Navy elements present did not commit themselves to the manifesto and made some of the Army, who had already given their support, hesitate and retreat. Even so, the document was approved at the end of the meeting by the majority of the officers present with 111 signatures in favour [19]. This was the first step towards the definition of a political programme that would support the change of regime and the transitional power structure that should take effect after the coup.

Otelo Saraiva de Carvalho recalled that this was the last major meeting of activists from the movement before the 25th of April and that it was especially relevant 'for the clarification of attitudes and the qualitative leap that it imprinted on the MFA.' In Cascais, they also approved the need to choose leaders for the MFA and the choice of Costa Gomes in first place and António Spínola in second, was ratified, as future military leaders of the regime that would emerge from a possible military operation triggered by the captains.[20]

When confronted with the choice of his name to be the head of the movement, Costa Gomes later replied that he knew nothing about the Cascais meeting and that he only became aware of it by chance.[21] He also said that he believed at the time, that regimes should evolve without coups d'état, as there was always the risk of 'a civil war with unpredictable consequences.'[22] While maintaining a certain ambiguity in relation to the activity of the captains, Costa Gomes considered that he at least did not denounce them, but he went on to say: 'I am fully convinced that if I were on the side of the government, the revolution would fail.'[23] Curiously, on the decisive day of the military coup, he was out of contact all day and later referred that he had been in the Military Hospital accompanying his wife, who was admitted there.[24]

At the Cascais meeting it was also decided to set up two working groups that would be in charge of 'planning and launching a military operation' and of 'reformulating the programme that would have to be submitted for review by the military chiefs.' The first group or 'military commission' consisted of Lieutenant-Colonel Amadeu Garcia dos Santos, Majors José Maria Azevedo, Otelo Saraiva de Carvalho and Manuel Monge, Captain Luís Macedo and Ensign Manuel Geraldes, who were later joined by Major Casanova Ferreira, recently returned from Guinea and later, by Captain Armando Ramos, representing the militia officers; the second group

Carlos Fabião (centre) and Otelo, at a military ceremony after 25 April 1974, when both held important positions in the military hierarchy. Both were part of the MFA military commission, in charge of planning and launching the operation to overthrow Caetano's government. (25th of April Association Collection)

Melo Antunes was part of the MFA political commission in charge of drawing up the political programme. Considered the main ideologist of the MFA, after the revolution, he was minister several times in the provisional governments, performing important functions. (Dutch National Archives)

or 'political commission' included Majors Melo Antunes, Vítor Alves and Captain Vasco Lourenço.

The movement also approved a vote of confidence in the Army Coordinating Commission and full support for the decisions it would take.

In addition, the military approved the suggestion to wait for the decision about the Air Force accession, which was to be presented on March 10, and to commit the Navy to present its decisions as soon as possible. It was also approved the constitution of a commission to be nominated by the Army Coordinating Commission, to analyse the forces in presence and propose concrete measures to implement the doctrine defined in the document. Vasco Lourenço, who was present at the meeting, noted that the military 'spinolists' had tried in this meeting to transform the MFA into a movement supporting the general, stating namely, that there was no need for a political programme, since they had a chief, which was Spínola. In response, Vasco Lourenço said that the leader chosen by the movement was Costa Gomes and not Spínola and Costa Gomes was eventually confirmed in a vote by a large majority, although Spínola was also included as the second leader.[25]

In this regard, Spínola revealed that both he and Costa Gomes knew what had happened at the meeting of the movement on 5 March and in subsequent meetings. However, he admits that only later did he learn about 'the manoeuvre of political involvement carried out in the Cascais meeting and which he considered a betrayal of the spirit of the captains' movement.' According to Spínola, two distinct currents emerged at this meeting, 'one consisting of military officers with prestige in Africa, who wanted immediate armed action to replace the government and to guarantee the solution to the overseas problem and to start the process of democratisation of the country, and the other represented by the officers who presided over the meeting' – Majors Vítor Alves and Melo Antunes and Captain Pinto Soares – who defended 'the extension of the movement of claims with the deliberate intention of politicising the military cadres who were not yet considered to be conveniently aware enough to accept the designs of a political revolution with Marxist roots.'[26]

This division between 'spinolists' and the others was also noted at the Cascais meeting by Melo Antunes when the question of 'who would be formally designated as the representative figure of the movement,' was discussed. Melo Antunes feared that this could lead to 'sufficient motives for division to abort joint efforts,' so he was prepared to hold several meetings with officers linked to General Spínola.

The distancing of some people from Spínola was not only explained by reservations regarding his personality but, above all, by the fact that his book – and presumably his political programme – did not really question the 'structures of the regime.' It limited itself to pointing out 'a political solution within the dictatorship itself,' that is, 'the constitution of a Portuguese community with its epicentre in Lisbon.'

The spinolist line, argues Melo Antunes, 'did not advocate a change of regime in the sense of effective democratisation, but rather proposed a certain liberalisation, which in fact presupposed the federation of the Portuguese space, as they understood it in imperial terms' but this did not mean 'such a radical regime change as we ended up imposing.'[27]

Vasco Lourenço was one of the most active elements of the MFA in the preparation of the military coup. After the revolution, he assumed important roles being appointed to the Council of State and later, to the Council of the Revolution, functions that he held until its extinction in 1982. (A Capital)

An agreement that never existed

With the discussion still going on in the National Assembly, but already knowing that the movement supported him, Spínola asked to be received by Marcello Caetano, which happened on the afternoon of 7 March and the account of the conversation was handwritten on seven small sheets now in Marcello Caetano's archives.[28]

According to this account, Spínola expressed to the President of the Council his regret for the trouble and concerns he had caused with the publication of the book, saying that 'the intention was good, just to help.' The book's author said he had heard the speech at the National Assembly (given two days earlier) and that in essence, he agreed with it. Marcello replied that the publication of the book 'had created serious difficulties for him and for the country, which is worse, both internally and internationally.' Spínola pointed out that in the long run, it would be useful and that he had received numerous messages of applause – even from members of parliament. Abroad, the reception was favourable even for him (President of the Council), as he was praised for allowing the publication and the existence of an agreement was admitted. The President of the Council replied: 'I might be pleased if the agreement had existed, but as it never existed, it is a misunderstanding.'

The problem, Caetano explained, was that when he published the book, he was still a military man and he was already in the second rank of the Armed Forces hierarchy. The result of the experience should have been put in a report to the President of the Council and the Minister of Overseas Territories, but to publish the book, hiding the text from the President of the Council, to whom he had become a direct collaborator, this, he did not understand. Marcello then referred to the current crisis: 'It is not my personal position that is at stake: but our functional situation. What would he think, if he were commander-in-chief, of one of his chiefs of staff who, without giving a hint, published a book in which he questioned his entire command action?' Marcello mentions that the general remained silent, but immediately afterwards he reaffirmed his loyalty. 'He wanted to tell me that he would never be a man of the left; whatever happened, they would never see him on the side of the opposition. He said he was a disciplined military man. He did not collaborate in revolutions. He is not a man of coups d'état.'

In spite of this, however, Spínola felt it was his duty to draw the attention of the Head of government to the situation in the Armed Forces. He said that the young officers of the permanent staff were still organised and dissatisfied, adding that they had sought him out and he considered it his duty to receive them because he considered it a mistake to lose contact with them. He received them in his office, in front of everyone, to exclude any suspicion of conspiracy and he had spoken to them in the clear language of discipline. 'Without discipline there is no army (…). In fact, I was aware that the so-called "organisation of captains" is still active. And I suspect that behind everything there is a desire not to fight any more [in the war]'. This is very serious, he concluded.

The effects of the book did not seem to give the government any more truce. The delegation in Mozambique of the DGS sent a letter on 9 March containing several considerations. Firstly, the book, which was published in the 23 February edition of the weekly newspaper *Expresso*, constituted a 'coup d'état on paper, with consequences in themselves more disastrous than terrorism overseas.' According to the same source, the book offered the prospect of a doubtful future, above all due to the present situation in which the performance of the Armed Forces was deficient and the military meddle in politics. It even mentioned that Spínola aspired to the government of the country, and for this, he accepted the position of deputy chief of the Armed Forces General Staff. For the Mozambican DGS, the author of the book accepted the position so that he could remain linked to the Armed Forces, through which he expected power to be taken in his favour.[29]

On 12 March another letter from Luís C. Lupi on the letterhead of *Lusitânia*, the news agency of the Portuguese press, enclosed two articles published in the English press: one from *The Daily Telegraph* (undated), another from the American magazine *Newsweek* of 11 March under the title 'How to stay in Africa' and another from *L'Express Afrique*, a French publication which spoke of fears in Africa concerning the development of the military situation.

The *Newsweek* article talked about the book's output and the opinion that Spínola conveyed in the work by advocating a political solution to the costly war in Africa. An advocate of partial independence, Spínola argued that this was the only way to maintain influence in Africa. He considered that the campaign of subversion and terror by the black guerrillas could not be crushed with weapons and that the solution was to confederate the Overseas Territories with governments endowed with great autonomy, in which the mainland would only deal with Finance, Defence and Foreign Affairs. If this solution was not implemented, Spínola predicted the rapid disintegration of the colonial empire. The magazine also said that 12 hours after publication, the book had sold out in kiosks in downtown Lisbon.

The article explained that the book had been well received by the regime's youth, who hailed the document as the most important in decades, but the dictatorship's right-wing had begun lobbying for Spínola's resignation. However, the regime of the conservative Marcello Caetano remained silent – it seemed possible that Caetano, having read the book previously, decided it had some merit.[30] In short, the American magazine article hinted that there may have been some complicity between Caetano and Spínola in the publication of the book, which was far from the truth as evidenced by the earlier conversation between Caetano and Spínola.

As for the article in *L'Express Afrique*, published on 11 February, it dealt with the unrest in Mozambique and the events in the city of Beira in early 1974, which had manifested themselves in protests by the white population against the military due to the expansion of the guerrillas. The article also referred to the appearance of surface-to-air missiles in the hands of the guerrillas, both in Guinea and Angola, although citing wrong information. The missiles mentioned in the article (SAM-3 and SAM-6) had never been supplied by the Soviets to any liberation movement in Africa and the Angolan guerrillas had no surface-to-air missiles, unlike the Guineans who used the SAM-7. The article also referred to some interventions by deputies in the National Assembly who questioned the evolution of the war in Mozambique and the fact that the enemy in Guinea was better armed than the Portuguese troops. The article ended by saying that in Portugal, there was a fact that was no longer a secret: the Army was starting to move.[31]

Compulsory transfers

Although the captains and other officers involved in the conspiracy were somewhat careful with the preparations, the truth was that the regime knew about some movements and began to act. On this issue, Melo Antunes confessed that there was some unawareness in the way the movement prepared the meetings, but also some cared not to give pretexts to the military hierarchy, the government and even PIDE/DGS to exercise a large-scale repressive action. Melo Antunes was, however, convinced that the political power would have no interest in repressing the movement on a large scale, given that it needed officers for the war in Africa and could not, therefore, exercise a punitive action that would deeply affect the Armed Forces. Moreover, the political culture of the PIDE/DGS was to persecute communist elements or African leaders linked to liberation movements and it was not in the habit of persecuting or monitoring military officers who were one of the mainstays of the regime.[32]

Vasco Lourenço had a slightly different opinion, believing that the political police were watching the movement and that for this reason, great care was taken when scheduling the meeting in Cascais on 5 March. The exact location of the meeting was known only to a very restricted group of people and only on the night of the meeting did the delegates of the various units find out that the meeting was in Cascais.[33]

Despite the precautions taken, Vasco Lourenço was caught with other colleagues in an exchange of correspondence that committed them to the movement. On 8 March, Captains Vasco Lourenço, Carlos Clemente, Antero Ribeiro da Silva and David Martelo were informed that they would be transferred to other units by ministerial order. The first two were to move to the Azores Independent Territorial Command, the third to the Madeira Independent Territorial Command and the last, from the Águeda Sergeants Central School (ECS), where he taught, to the Battalion 3, in Bragança. That same day, Otelo Saraiva de Carvalho was informed of what had happened. In his reading, the authorities, having learnt of the Cascais meeting, were moving to try and destroy the movement.

Unaware of the reasons for the government's decision, the movement understood that the really important person in the organisation was Vasco Lourenço, a member of the direction and the driving force behind the connection. Carlos Clemente and David Martelo were delegates and activists, without management functions and Antero Silva was a liaison officer. All three were easily replaceable, but Vasco Lourenço had important roles.[34]

To show displeasure with the transfer decision, the movement decided to prevent the captains' embarkation to the Azores and Madeira by simulating a type of kidnapping and also, to hold a demonstration in front of the Ministry of the Army. However, some members of the Navy suggested speaking to the Minister of the Navy, Pereira Crespo, to see if he could convince the Minister of the Army to revoke the order. Contacts were made to that effect, but Pereira Crespo refused to put any pressure on the Army Minister and then alerted the Minister of Defence as to the gravity of the situation, which led the minister to take measures.[35] On the following day, 9 March, the Armed Forces went into strict lockdown and all officers on duty were obliged to remain in their units, which made any protest impossible.[36]

On the government side, the under-secretary of State for the Army, Viana de Lemos, justified the officers' transfer. Captain Vasco Lourenço had been incriminated in a case filed by the Army General Staff (EME), since he had been the bearer of a large number of anonymous pamphlets, related to a demonstration of solidarity by officers from metropolitan Portugal with their comrades from Mozambique involved in the incidents that had taken place in Beira. Viana de Lemos said that it would be convenient for him to stay away from the mainland until the situation had calmed down.[37]

Almost simultaneously, the under-secretary of State reported, he became aware of copies of the movement's documents. In one of them, which he said he had become aware of in early March, he noted that the movement was being organised by Arms and Military Regions and established the liaison cells. The document in question referred to the Infantry and to the Military Region of Coimbra and indicated as responsible for the network, Captain Carlos Clemente and in his absence, Captain Ribeiro da Silva. It also mentioned the names of the officers delegated to the different Infantry units in the Military Region of Coimbra and ended with the indication that it should be destroyed after being read. In another, which was entirely handwritten, there was talk of a dinner in honour of Major Hugo dos Santos, financial contributions to the movement and the need to contact lieutenant-colonels and colonels. In this case, also, it was decided to move to the neighbouring islands.

Kidnapping and abduction

On the eve of 8 March, the date scheduled for the embarkation of the three officers, there was, in the opinion of the under-secretary of State, the first open rebellion with an incident of 'kidnapping and abduction' of two of those officers who, the following day, were delivered by Captain Pinto Soares to the Headquarters of the Military Region of Lisbon. Viana relates that it all began in the early hours of March 8 when he was alerted by the Minister of the Navy and then by the Secretary of State for Aeronautics, who told him they had been warned that a movement or a meeting of officers was being prepared to prevent the transfers. At dawn that morning, for the first time, all the ministers of the military sectors met in the Army Minister's office and precautions were taken to ensure the shipments, but it turned out that only Captain Clemente showed up on the 9th.[38] In Otelo Saraiva de Carvalho's version, Captain Carlos Clemente did not appear voluntarily. What happened was that at 6:30 in the morning of the 9th, Lieutenant-Colonel Ferrand d'Almeida knocked on Carlos Clemente's door saying he had orders to take him to his unit, RC 7, and keep him there until he could be accompanied to the plane that would take him to the Azores.[39]

Back at the ministerial meeting, Viana de Lemos noted that during the session the Defence Minister tried for 40 minutes to alert General Costa Gomes, who only showed up on the morning of the 9th, claiming that he had not heard the phone because he had taken a sleeping pill. According to Viana, Costa Gomes first considered the transfers unjustified, but then remained silent when he showed him the pamphlets. It should be noted that there is nothing about this meeting in the archives of the military ministers. Viana Lemos also confesses that, despite several inquiries he made in the following days to regiment commanders and even to two generals who were more responsible for the Army's fate, he was unable to understand what the movement's real goals were, which would have been fundamental to guide his action [40] .

As previously mentioned, Vasco Lourenço and Ribeiro da Silva eventually surrendered at the headquarters of the Lisbon Military Region on the night of 9 to 10 March, led by Captain Pinto Soares,

In 1974, Marcello Caetano was increasingly an isolated ruler with no political solutions to the crisis affecting the Portuguese armed forces. (A Capital)

who was in solidarity with the two captains and who had submitted his resignation as an Army officer for not agreeing with the transfers. As a result of this action, the three were imprisoned at the Trafaria Fort for six days, after which, Vasco Lourenço was taken to Ponta Delgada in the Azores and Ribeiro da Silva to Funchal, on the island of Madeira.[41] The only one who managed to escape the penalty was David Martelo, thanks to the influence of the Águeda ECS commander, who did everything in his power to ensure that the young captain was not transferred to Bragança as planned.[42]

However, all this military unrest was exposed in the pages of the English newspaper *Financial Times* through an article by Bruce Loudon. The English correspondent in Lisbon, reporting from the Portuguese capital on 12 March, reported the crisis in the Army and the rebellion of the young officers who were unhappy with their professional situation and who saw in Spínola 'their hero and their hope.' The journalist described the military moves to prevent the transfers of the four punished officers and the imposition of a state of alert by the government. Bruce Loudon also mentions that some officers demanded the resignation of the Minister of the Army, Andrade e Silva and the Minister of Defence, Silva Cunha, and that Spínola's position had been strengthened by this crisis, since it was highly unlikely that the government would want to further anger the young officers by dismissing Spínola.

According to the journalist, there were those who wanted Caetano to take over the area of Defence and to nominate Spínola or Costa Gomes as Minister of the Army, but that this intention could come into conflict with the President of the Republic, who was against Spínola and Costa Gomes.[43] Anyone who read the article could perfectly understand the conspiratorial climate that reigned in the Army. Marcello Caetano was increasingly an isolated ruler without political solutions to the crisis affecting the military forces.

SOURCES AND BIBLIOGRAPHY

Sources

Archives du MAE
General Directorate of Archives (DGARQ)
Historical Archive of the Presidency of the Republic (AHPR)
Historical Diplomatic Archive (AHD)
Marcello Caetano Archive (AMC)
Military Historical Archive (AHM)
National Archive of Torre do Tombo (ANTT)
National Archives, Washington D.C.
National Defence Archive (ADN)
Overseas Historical Archive (AHU)
Presidency of the Republic Museum – António de Spínola Archive (MPR/AAS)

Documentaries

Furtado, Joaquim, A Guerra, RTP 2008, 42 episodes.
Pontes, Joana, A Hora da Liberdade, SIC 1999.

Press

Several newspapers and magazines were consulted in the research for this book.

A Capital
Diário de Notícias
Diário Popular
Expresso
Flama
Jornal de Macau
L'Express Afrique
Le Figaro
Le Monde
Mais Alto
Manchete
Newsweek
O Dia
O Mundo Português
O Referencial
O Seculo Ilustrado
Publico
Rand Daily Mail
República
Sempre Fixe
Tal & Qual
The Daily Telegraph
The Sunday Telegraph
The Financial Times
Washington Star News

Bibliography

AAVV, *25 de Abril, Os 240 que prenderam Caetano, A coluna militar da EPC*, (Lisbon: Special edition Público, 25 April 1999)

Abreu, Paradela, *Do 25 de Abril ao 25 de Novembro: memória do tempo perdido*, (Lisbon: Intervenção, 1983)

Abreu, Paradela de (Coord.), *Os Últimos Governadores do Império*, (Lisbon: Edições Neptuno, 1994)

Almeida, Dinis, *Origens e evolução do Movimento de Capitães: subsídios para uma melhor compreensão*, (Lisbon: Ed.Sociais, 1977)

Almeida, Luís Pinheiro e Cabral, Rui, *25 de Abril, memórias*, (Lisbon: Agência Lusa, special edition, 1994)

Amaral, Diogo Freitas do, *O Antigo Regime e a Revolução Memórias Políticas (1941–1975)*, (Venda Nova: Edições Bertrand/Nomen, 1995)

Andrade, Nuno, *Para Além do Portão. A GNR e o Carmo na Revolução de Abril*, (Lisbon: Guerra e Paz, 2007)

Antunes, José Freire, *Os Americanos e Portugal* Vol. I *Os anos de Richard Nixon 1969–1974*, (Lisbon: Publicações Dom Quixote, 1986)

Antunes, José Freire, *Os Americanos e Portugal. Nixon e Caetano: Promessas e Abandono – 1969–1974*, (Lisbon: Difusão Cultural, 1992)

Antunes, José Freire, *A Guerra de África*, Volume II (Lisbon: Círculo de Leitores, 1995)

Arriaga, Kaúlza de, *Guerra e Política: Em nome da Verdade, Os Anos Decisivos*, 2ª edition, (Lisbon: Edições Referendo, 1987)

Azeredo, Carlos de, *Trabalhos e Dias de Um Soldado do Império*, (Porto: Livraria Civilização Editora, 2004)

Baptista, Jacinto, *Caminhos para uma Revolução*, (Amadora: Livraria Bertrand, 1975)

Barroso, José Manuel, *Segredos de Abril*, (Lisbon: Editorial Notícias, 1995)

Bernardo, Manuel, *Marcello e Spínola: A Ruptura. As Forças Armadas e a Imprensa na Queda do Estado Novo, 1973–1974*, (Lisbon: Edições Margem, 1999)

Bernardo, Manuel, *Equívocos e Realidades – Portugal 1974–1975*, Vol. I (Lisbon: Nova Arrancada, 1999)

Bernardo, Joaquim Manuel Correia, *Santarém. Uma cidade que faz História. 25 de Abril de 1974*, (Santarém: Research Centre Professor Doutor Joaquim Veríssimo Serrão, 2015)

Boyer-Peter, *Winds of Destruction* (Pinetown: 30º South Publishers, 2005)

Brito, Carlos, *Álvaro Cunhal Sete fôlegos de um combatente*, (Lisbon: Edições Nelson de Matos, 2010)

Caetano, Marcello, *Depoimento*, (Rio de Janeiro: Distribuidora Record, 1974)

Caetano, Marcello, *O 25 de Abril e o Ultramar. Três entrevistas e alguns documentos*, (Lisbon: Verbo, 1977)

Caio, Horácio, *Guiné 74 – Vigilância e Resposta*, (Lisbon: 1974)

Cardoso, José Armando Vizela, *Voando no céu do reino de Monomotapa. Guerra do Ultramar. Moçambique 1972–1974*, (Porto: Fronteira do Caos, 2016)

Carvalho, Otelo Saraiva de, *Alvorada em Abril*, (Lisbon: Bertrand, 1977)

Carvalho, Otelo Saraiva de, *O dia inicial. 25 de Abril. Hora a Hora*, (Lisbon: Editora Objectiva, 2011)

Charais, Franco, *História Viva – 25 de Abril: Golpe Militar ou Revolução?*, (Lisbon: Âncora Editora, 2013)

Castanheira, José Pedro, 'O livro que abalou o regime' *Expresso* magazine n.º 1112, 19 February 1994

Castanheira, José Pedro, 'A reunião que veio tarde demais,' *Expresso* magazine n.º 1117, 26 March 1994

Castanheira, José Pedro, 'Conversas em Roma,' *Expresso* magazine n.º 1226, 27 April 1996

Central Intelligence Bulletin, March 15, 1974, CIA-RDP-79T00975A026200200001-8, CIA Records Search Tool (CREST), National Archives and Records Administration

Chenel, Bernard [et al.], *Mirage III/5/50 en service à l` étranger*, (Le Vigen: Lela Presse, 2014)

Contreiras, Carlos de Almada [et al.], *Operação Viragem Histórica: 25 de Abril de 1974*, 2ª edition, (Lisbon: Edições Colibri, 2018)

Costa Gomes sobre Portugal – Diálogos com Alexandre Manuel, (Lisbon: A Regra do Jogo, 1979)

Costeira, Arnaldo, *Eu Capitão de Abril me confesso*, (Porto: Lello Editores, 1999)

Crespo, Manuel Pereira, *Porque Perdemos a Guerra*, (Edições Abril, 1977)

Cruz, Manuel Braga da, Ramos, Rui (org.), *Marcello Caetano – Tempos de Transição*, (Porto: Porto Editora, 2012)

Cruzeiro, Maria Manuela, *Costa Gomes: O último marechal*, (Lisbon: Editorial Notícias, 1998)

Cruzeiro, Maria Manuela, *Melo Antunes, O sonhador pragmático*, 3ª edition, (Lisbon: Editorial de Notícias, 2005)

Cruzeiro, Maria Manuela, *Vasco Lourenço do Interior da Revolução*, (Lisbon: Âncora Editora, 2009)

Cunha, Silva, *O Ultramar, a Nação e o 25 de Abril*, (Coimbra: Atlântida Editora, 1977)

Cunha, Silva, *Ainda o 25 de Abril*, (Lisbon: Centro do Livro Brasileiro, 1984)

Cunha, Alfredo, Gomes, Adelino, *Os rapazes dos tanques, (*Porto: Porto Editora, 2014)

Folques, Raul, 'Os Comandos na Guiné,' (Lisbon: magazine *'Mama Sume,'* N.º 64, 2006, pp.13–20)

Frazão, António e Filipe, Maria do Céu Barata, *Arquivo Marcello Caetano*, Volumes I e II, (Lisbon: Instituto dos Arquivos Nacionais/Torre do Tombo, 2005)

Golias, Jorge Sales, *A Descolonização da Guiné-Bissau e o Movimento dos Capitães*, 2ª edition, (Lisbon: Edições Colibri, 2017)

Gomes, Bernardino e Sá, Tiago Moreira de, *Carlucci vs Kissinger – Os EUA e a revolução portuguesa,* (Lisbon: Dom Quixote, 2008)

Hernandez, Humberto C. Trujillo, *El Grito del Baobab*, (Habana: Editorial de Ciencias Sociales, 2008)

Jardim, Jorge, *Moçambique – Terra Queimada*, (Lisbon: Editorial Intervenção, 1976)

Júnior, J. Plácido, *25 de Abril: A história nunca contada dos três azarados da coluna de Salgueiro Maia*, magazine 'Visão,' May 1, 2021

Lã, João Rosa, *Do Outro Lado das Coisas – (In)Confidências Diplomáticas*, 3ª edition, (Santa Cruz: Book Builders/Letras Errantes, 2015)

Lauret, Pedro, *O Dia da Liberdade. 25 de Abril de 1974*, (Vila do Conde: Verso da História, 2015)

Lemos, Mário Matos e, *O 25 de Abril – Uma síntese, uma perspectiva*, (Lisbon: Editorial Notícias, 1986)

Lemos, Viana de, *Duas Crises, 1961 e 1974 – um olhar de um oficial do exército português*, 2ª edition, (Lisbon: Edições Cosmos, 2009)

Loudon, Bruce, 'Portuguese forces put on alert,' *The Sunday Telegraph*, March 10, 1974.

Loudon, Bruce, 'Africa War Crisis Grips Portugal,' *The Daily Telegraph*, March 11, 1974.

Loudon, Bruce, 'Portuguese Cabinet shake-up likely in bid to defuse army crisis,' *The Financial Times*, March 13, 1974

Loudon, Bruce, 'How the mighty pen split Portugal,' *The Sunday Telegraph*, March 17, 1974

Magalhães, J. Calvet de, *O 25 de Abril e as necessidades*, (Lisbon: Estratégia – Revista de Estudos Internacionais, IEEI, 2004)

Maia, Matos, *Aqui Emissora da Liberdade: Rádio Clube Português 04.26 25 de Abril de 1974*, (Lisbon: Edição Rádio Clube Português, 1975)

Maia, Salgueiro, *Capitão de Abril. Histórias da Guerra do Ultramar e do 25 de Abril*, (Lisbon: Notícias Editorial, 1997)

Manuel, Alexandre, Carapinha, Rogério, Neves, Dias (eds.), *PIDE: a história da repressão,* (Fundão: Jornal do Fundão, 1974)

Marques, Silvino Silvério, *Portugal, e agora?*, (Lisbon: Edições do Templo, 1978)

Marques, Silvino Silvério, *Marcello Caetano, Angola e o 25 de Abril – Uma Polémica com Veríssimo Serrão*, (Mem Martins: Editorial Inquérito, 1995)

Matos, José, *História secreta dos Mirages portugueses*, Mais Alto n.º 400 (Nov/Dec 2012) e Mais Alto n.º 401(Jan/Feb 2013)

Matos, José, Barroso, Luís, *Nos Meandros da Guerra – O Estado Novo e a África do Sul na Defesa da Guiné*, (Lisbon: Caleidoscópio, 2020)

Mello, Manuel José Homem de, *Meio Século de Observação*, (Lisbon: Círculo de Leitores, 1996)

Miller, J., Things fall apart: South Africa and the collapse of the Portuguese Empire, 1973–74. *Cold War History*, 12:2, 2012, pp.183–204

Monteiro, Pedro, *Berliet, Chaimite e UMM – Os Grandes Veículos Militares Nacionais*,
(Lisbon: Contra a Corrente, 2018)

Monteiro, Fábio, *Esquecidos em Abril – Os mortos da revolução sem sangue*, (Lisbon: Livros Horizonte, 2019)

Moura, Paulo, *Otelo – O Revolucionário*, (Lisbon: Publicações Dom Quixote, 2012)

Morais, Carlos Alexandre de, *António de Spínola – O Homem*, (Lisbon: Editorial Estampa, 2007)

Múrias, Manuel Maria, *De Salazar a Costa Gomes*, (Lisbon: Nova Arrancada, 1998)

Ockrent, Christine, Marenches, Conde de, *No Segredo dos Deuses*, (Lisbon: Edições Referendo, 1988)

Oliveira, Zélia Costa de, *Os 63 dias que abalaram o Estado Novo – Incursão histórica à crise terminal do regime*, Master thesis, (Lisbon: Nova University, 2012)

Osório, Sanches, *O Equívoco do 25 de Abril*, (Lisbon: Editorial Intervenção, 1975)

Pereira, António Maria, *A Burla do 28 de Setembro*, (Lisbon: Livraria Bertrand, 1976)

Pinto, Pedro Feytor, *Na Sombra do Poder*, (Lisbon: Publicações D. Quixote, 2011)

Pontes, Joana, Castro, Rodrigo de Sousa e, Afonso, Aniceto, *A Hora da Liberdade. O 25 de Abril, pelos protagonistas*, (Lisbon: Editorial Bizâncio, 2012)

Pronunciamento Militar do 25 de Abril de 1974, V Conferência do Núcleo Impulsionador das Conferências da Cooperativa Militar (NICCM), (Lisbon: Edição NICCM, 2014)

Rebello, Augusto de Sá Viana, *Salazar e Caetano Falar Claro*, (Lisbon: Nova Arrancada, 2003)

Rocha, João Manuel, 'Guiné-Bissau – Os camaradas estão a perguntar se é assim que se toma a independência,' *Público*, 24 September 2013

Rodrigues, Paulo Madeira, *De Súbito em Abril, 24, 25, 26*, (Lisbon: Arcádia, 1974)

Rosas, Fernando (Direção) e Brito, J. M. Brandão, *Dicionário de História do Estado Novo*, Volume II, (Lisbon: Círculo de Leitores, 1996)

Santos, Bruno Oliveira, *Histórias Secretas da PIDE/DGS*, (Lisbon: Nova Arrancada, 2000)

Santos, Garcia dos [et al.], *As transmissões militares: Da Guerra Peninsular ao 25 de Abril*, (Lisbon: Comissão da História das Transmissões, 2008)

Serrão, Joaquim Veríssimo, *Marcello Caetano - Confidências no Exílio*, (Lisbon: Editorial Verbo, 1985)

Serrão, Joaquim Veríssimo, *Correspondência com Marcello Caetano - 1974–1980*, (Venda Nova: Bertrand Editora, 1994)

Sieve, Harold, 'Portuguese 'coup' ends in fiasco.' *The Sunday Telegraph*, March 17, 1974

Sieve, Harold, 'Portuguese purge of armed forces continues.' *The Daily Telegraph*, March 19, 1974

Sieve, Harold, 'Purge of Portuguese Army extended.' *The Daily Telegraph*, March 20, 1974

Silva, Alexandre Pais Ribeiro da, *Capitães de Abril*, Vol. I, (Lisbon: Amigos do Livro, Editores, 1974)

Soares, Mário, *Um político assume-se, Ensaio autobiográfico político e ideológico*, (Lisbon: Temas e Debates/Círculo de Leitores, 2011)

Sousa, Pedro Marquês de, *Os Números da Guerra de África – Angola Guiné e Moçambique*, (Lisbon: Guerra e Paz, 2021)

Spínola, António de, *Portugal e o Futuro*, 5ª edition (Lisbon: Arcádia, 1974)

Spínola, António de, *País sem rumo - Contributo para a História de uma Revolução*, (Lisbon: SCIRE, 1978)

Swift, Kerry, *Mozambique and the future*, (Cape Town: Don Nelson, 1974)

Tal, David, *Symbol Not Substance? Israel's Campaign to Acquire Hawk Missiles, 1960–1962*, The International History Review Vol. 22, No. 2 (Jun. 2000)

Tavares-Teles, António, *Otelo - 18 de Janeiro*, (Lisbon: Edição de autor, 1976)

Themido, João Hall, *Dez anos em Washington,1971–1981*, (Lisbon: Dom Quixote, 1995)

Thomaz, Américo, *Últimas décadas de Portugal*, Vol. IV, (Lisbon: Fernando Pereira Editor, 1983)

Tíscar, Maria José, *A Pide no Xadrez Africano - Conversas com o inspector Fragoso Allas*, 2ª edition, (Lisbon: Edições Colibri, 2018)

Tornada, Joana de Matos, *Nas vésperas da democracia em Portugal, o golpe das Caldas de 16 de março*, (Coimbra: Almedina, 2009)

Ulanoff, Stanley M. e Eshel, David, *The Fighting Israeli Air Force - The Amazing Combat History of the World´s Finest Air Force 1948–1984*, (New York: Arco Publishing, INC, 1985)

Vasco, Nuno, *Vigiados e perseguidos. Documentos Secretos da PIDE/DGS*, (Amadora: Livraria Bertrand, 1977)

Vieira, Joaquim, *Mário Soares, uma vida* (revised and extended biography), volume II (Sábado magazine), (Lisbon: Reverso, 2022)

Villas-Boas, José Manuel, *Caderno de Memórias*, (Lisbon: Temas e Debates, 2003)

Wery, Max, *E assim murcharam os cravos*, (Lisbon: Editorial Fragmentos, 1994)

NOTES

Introduction

1 On this issue, see Almeida, Dinis, *Origens e evolução do Movimento de Capitães: subsídios para uma melhor compreensão,* 2nd edition (Lisbon: Ed.Sociais, 1977), pp.98–112.

2 Caetano, Marcello, *Depoimento*, (Rio de Janeiro: Distribuidora Record,1974), pp.186–188.

3 Spínola, António de, *Portugal e o Futuro*, 5th Edition, (Lisbon: Arcádia, 1974), pp.160–162.

4 Caetano, *Depoimento*, p.196.

5 Carvalho, Otelo Saraiva de, *Alvorada em Abril*, (Lisbon: Bertrand, 1977), pp.232. The proposal was part of a manifesto read by Melo Antunes that night, which recognised the right of the African peoples to govern themselves. The manifesto, however, raised doubts among those present and led several military officers not to support the proposal.

6 AHM/DIV/1/39/4/12: Processo sobre o 'Incidente das Caldas em 16 de Março de 1974.'

7 Carvalho, *Alvorada em Abril*, pp.276–277.

8 Salgueiro Maia's interview with Adelino Gomes published in the supplement of no. 664 of the magazine *Fatos e Fotos*, May 1974.

9 Caetano acknowledged in a radio and television intervention on 'The paths to the future of Overseas Territories,' on 15 January 1973, reproduced in *Razões da Presença de Portugal no Ultramar* (Lisbon: 1973), p.91, that the revision of the organic law for Overseas Territories had provoked discontent in some overseas sectors that expected more, but that he did not, however, find serious reasons for this discontent.

10 According to Pedro Feytor Pinto, who was director of the Information Services of the Secretariat of State for Information and Tourism, Marcello Caetano was against a white independence, as had happened in Rhodesia, but he also refused to negotiate with the liberation movements. Caetano advocated a 'third way' which involved the formation of a ruling class of whites, blacks, and mestizos, native to the territory, who would one day assume responsibilities of governance in future independent states. Cf. Pinto, Pedro Feytor, *Na Sombra do Poder*, (Lisbon: Publicações D. Quixote, 2011), p.225.

11 According to Otelo, many of the officers who served in Guinea were convinced that the government in Portugal wanted to abandon the colony to concentrate its efforts in Angola and that the best way to leave, without negotiating with the rebels, was with a military defeat, blaming the military for what had happened. See Tavares-Teles, António, *Otelo - 18 de Janeiro*, (Lisbon: Author's Edition, 1976), pp.304–305.

12 In an interview with Maria Manuela Cruzeiro, Costa Gomes seems to agree with this theory by stating that 'the first overseas province to make peace would drag the others that were at war into an identical movement.' For Costa Gomes it was evident that having peace in Guinea, Portuguese troops would lose the will to fight in Angola and Mozambique, 'as they would always keep in mind the possibility of a resolution of the colonial problem through

negotiations.' Cf. Cruzeiro, Maria Manuela, *Costa Gomes: O último marechal*, (Lisbon: Editorial Notícias, 1998), p.167.

13 Caetano, Marcello, *O 25 de Abril e o Ultramar. Três entrevistas e alguns documentos*, (Lisbon: Verbo, s.d.), p.103. The letter is digitised in Spínola's archive at the Museum of the Presidency of the Republic. https://www.arquivo.museu.presidencia.pt/details?id=164819.

14 MPR/AAS/CX000/0270: Letter from António de Spínola to António Ramalho Eanes explaining the reasons for writing 'Portugal and the Future,' 19 April 1974.

15 Archives du MAE, FR MAE 200QO, Direction Europe, Portugal, Relations politiques franco-portugaises, 186–191, Visite à Paris de Rui Patrício, ministre portugais des Affaires étrangères, les 7 et 8 janvier 1974, 187, série 28, sous série 24, dossier 1, Directeur des Affaires Politiques, note pour le ministre, 8 janvier 1974.

16 Villas-Boas, José Manuel, *Caderno de Memórias*, (Lisbon: Temas e Debates, 2003).

17 Pinto, *Na Sombra do Poder*, p.260.

Chapter 1

1 AHPR/GB/GB0205/1729/111: Supreme Council of National Defence – Report of the session of 15 February 1974.

2 MPR/AAS/0253: Note on the conversation between Spínola and Marcello Caetano at the Council Presidency on 8 May 1969, p.3.

3 Sousa, Pedro Marquês de, *Os Números da Guerra* de *África – Angola Guiné e Moçambique*, (Lisbon: Guerra e Paz, 2021), p.106, analyses the number of deaths per thousand soldiers in service in the Army, in each year. However, in a 10-year analysis (1964–1973), it is observed that Guinea had the highest average (8.2), followed by Mozambique (6.6) and Angola (4.4), a sign that in that colony, the war was more deadly over time.

4 The comment refers to the purchase, in France, of two platoons of Crotale R 440 missiles, the first one to be delivered in May 1974 and the second 18 months later. Cunha, Silva, *O Ultramar, a Nação e o 25 de Abril*, (Coimbra: Atlântida Editora, 1977), p.318. The missiles would be purchased in France and would arrive in Portugal in September 1974, after the war was over. Thus, it was decided to return the system to the French. The Portuguese order signed in January 1974 had a total value of 91 million French francs. See ADN/GABMIN/007/0036/053.

5 In a summary note on the visit to France by the Portuguese Minister of Foreign Affairs, Rui Patrício, in January 1974, the French calculated that arms sales to Portugal during the 1960s amounted to 800 million francs, and that in 1971 and 1972, they had stabilised at around 61 million francs. In these last two years, Portugal was ranked 12th and 15 in the lists of French exports of war material. Cf. Archives du MAE, FR MAE 200QO, Direction Europe, Portugal, Relations politiques franco-portugaises, 186–191, Visite à Paris de Rui Patrício, ministre portugais des Affaires étrangères, les 7 et 8 janvier 1974, 187, série 28, sous série 24, dossier 1, note de synthèse, Les ventes d`armes au Portugal, pp.11–12.

6 The Fiat G.91 had been supplied by West Germany in 1965 under special conditions, but the Germans were now refusing to supply new aircraft in order not to commit themselves to the Portuguese colonial war. Portugal had three Fiat squadrons in Africa, with one in Guinea and two in Mozambique.

7 This information was correct. In fact, Zaire had signed on 20 September 1973 a contract with the French for the acquisition of 14 Mirage 5M and three Mirage DM, which were to be delivered from 1975. Chenel, Bernard et al. *Mirage III/5/50 en service à l` étranger*, (Le Vigen: Lela Presse, 2014), p.304.

8 The Mirage was a supersonic fighter with superior performance to the Fiat G.91 or the Aermacchi MB-326, a light training and attack aircraft. In addition, the Mirage could perform air defence functions against enemy fighters and was a fighter with greater weapons capacity and longer combat radius than the Fiat G.91.

9 A principal agreement had been reached in Pretoria at the end of 1973, with the South Africans agreeing to a loan of 150 million rands, which would then be materialised in an agreement between both countries, in March 1974. AHD – PAA 960, 18 Packet 1140: Telegram No. 363 from the Portuguese Embassy in Pretoria, 11 December 1973.

10 In a series of interviews he gave to Alexandre Manuel in 1979, Costa Gomes stated that he always considered military victory in Africa impossible, however, in the meetings of the Higher Council of National Defence (CSDN) in which he took part, we found that he never expressed this opinion to those present. Cf. *Costa Gomes sobre Portugal – Diálogos com Alexandre Manuel*, (Lisbon: A Regra do Jogo, 1979), p.33. However, in a later interview in 1994 to Lusa News Agency, he stated that he had defended in the CSDN that it was necessary to find a political solution to the war and that Marcello Caetano had given orders to the secretary of the CSDN not to include this opinion of Costa Gomes in the council's records. Almeida, Luís Pinheiro and Cabral, Rui, *25 de Abril, memórias*, (Lisbon: Agência Lusa, special edition, 1994), p. 84. In an interview with Maria Manuela Cruzeiro, he again insists on this point and stresses that the records have been destroyed. Cf. Cruzeiro, *Costa Gomes: O ultimo marechal*, p.162. From our research in the Presidency's Archives, we found that at least three records of the meetings were missing from the CSDN inventory and that they were certainly destroyed at the time of the 25th of April Revolution.

11 Caetano, *Depoimento*, p.196.

12 Carvalho, *Alvorada em Abril*, p.215. In the biography written by Paulo Moura, *Otelo – O Revolucionário*, (Lisbon: Publicações Dom Quixote, 2012), pp.187–188, this conversation is reproduced differently. Spínola is apparently said to Otelo the following: 'Do you want to know something? Marcello Caetano won't let me publish my book (...) I gave him a copy and he says that I cannot publish it, because it advocates a policy completely opposite to that of the Government.' And he adds: 'Chico (Francisco Costa Gomes) is with me, man. He's already given the green light for publication. Marcello is the one who says he will resign if I publish it.' This version of the conversation finds no support in other sources, not even in the book that Otelo wrote in 1977.

13 Caetano, *Depoimento*, pp.189–190.

14 Cunha, *O Ultramar, a Nação e o 25 de Abril*, p.48.

15 It was not possible to find the minutes of this meeting in archives, but they are published in Tíscar, Maria José, *A Pide no Xadrez Africano – Conversas com o inspector Fragoso Allas*, 2nd edition, (Lisbon: Edições Colibri, 2018), pp.306–313.

16 Testimony of António de Spínola in Abreu, Paradela de (Coord.), *Os Últimos Governadores do Império*, (Lisbon: Edições Neptuno, 1994), pp.73–74.

17 Spínola, António de, *País sem rumo – Contributo para a História de uma Revolução*, (Lisbon: SCIRE, 1978), p.46.

18 Vasco Lourenço, who was one of the captains of April, tells Maria Manuela Cruzeiro in an interview that the book was written by Major Pereira da Costa, who was Spínola's assistant and who wrote the general's speeches. Spínola would have given him ideas, but it was Pereira da Costa who wrote the book. Cf. *Vasco Lourenço do Interior da Revolução*, interview by Maria Manuela Cruzeiro,

(Lisbon: Âncora Editora, 2009), pp.162–163. This idea is shared by Costa Gomes, who also claims that Pereira da Costa wrote the book, although the ideas had been provided by Spínola. Cruzeiro, *Costa Gomes: O último marechal*, p.150. Spínola himself recognises that Pereira da Costa had an important role in the preparation of the book. However, other collaborators of Spínola in Guinea also made their contributions, which shows that the work was collective with contributions from several officers connected to Spínola. Cf. Castanheira, José Pedro, *Expresso* Magazine no. 1112, 19 February 1994, pp.38–39.

19 Abreu, Paradela, *Do 25 de Abril ao 25 de Novembro: memória do tempo perdido*, (Lisbon: Intervenção, 1983), pp.29–31.

20 Abreu, *Do 25 de Abril ao 25 de Novembro*, pp.34–39.

21 *República*, 22 February 1974, p.24.

22 *Expresso*, 23 February 1974.

23 In an interview with Maria Manuela Cruzeiro, Costa Gomes reveals that it was he who suggested to Caetano the creation of this post, which until then, had not existed, to accommodate Spínola after his return from Guinea. Cf. Cruzeiro, *Costa Gomes: O último marechal*, p.168.

24 Cunha, Silva, *Ainda o 25 de Abril*, (Lisbon: Centro do Livro Brasileiro, 1984), p.98.

25 Spínola, *País sem rumo*, pp.72–73.

26 Justification for allowing the book to come out, according to Miguel Caetano, son of Marcello Caetano, interviewed by Zélia Oliveira in March 2012.

27 ADN/CEMGFA/032/0068/002: Opinion no. 04245/GC of 11 February 1974 issued by CEMGFA. Subject: Portugal and the Future. Costa Gomes's opinion does not mention the first part of the book, which was the one that really bothered Caetano and made the headlines in the *República* newspaper.

28 In an interview with Maria Manuela Cruzeiro, Vasco Lourenço tells that Costa Gomes gave the book to the staff of his office to read. One of the readers was Admiral António Tierno *Bagulho*, who was Assistant Secretary of National Defence and a personal friend of Spínola. After reading the book he said to Spínola: 'Oh António, but you are not in the book. This is not you,' confirming the idea that Spínola had not written the book. *Vasco Lourenço do Interior da Revolução*, interview by Maria Manuela Cruzeiro, (Lisbon: Âncora Editora, 2009), p.163. In an interview with Lusa News Agency in 1994, Costa Gomes confirmed that he gave his assent to the book in order to launch the debate on the overseas question in public opinion, a subject that was taboo until then. Almeida e Cabral, *25 de Abril, memórias*, p.84.

29 Thomaz, *Últimas Décadas de Portugal*, pp.351–352.

30 Cunha, *Ainda o 25 de Abril*, pp.99–101.

31 Cruzeiro, Maria Manuela, *Costa Gomes: O último marechal*, (Lisbon: Editorial Notícias, 1998), p.189. In the series of interviews, he gave to Maria Manuela Cruzeiro, Costa Gomes states that he always maintained that war did not solve the problem of Overseas Territories and that the solution was political, p.190. However, as we said before, in the meetings of the Supreme Council of National Defence in which he participated he never expressed that opinion. Silva Cunha also stated that he never heard Costa Gomes raise any doubts as to the possibility of continuing to defend the Overseas Territories. Cf. Cunha, *Ainda o 25 de Abril*, p.58.

32 It seems, however, that before it was published, the book was already circulating in the Lisbon journalistic environment. Jacinto Baptista, who worked at the *Diário Popular* newspaper, confesses in his memoirs that he had access to a copy of the book with notes from the author himself, weeks before the work was published. After leafing through the book, he immediately understood that '*Portugal e o Futuro*' was, in fact, an unparalleled event, not so much because of what was said in it, but because of who said it, in accordance with an ideology and a desire of action that were being developed semi-clandestinely and that would find in António de Spínola's work, its first great public projection (...)'. Baptista, Jacinto, *Caminhos para uma Revolução*, (Amadora: Livraria Bertrand, 1975), pp.184–185.

33 Rebello, Augusto de Sá Viana, *Salazar e Caetano Falar Claro*, (Lisbon: Nova Arrancada, 2003), p.182.

34 MPR/AAS/CX000/0252: António de Spínola's essay, entitled 'Algumas ideias sobre a estruturação política da Nação' (Some ideas on the Nation's political structure), October 1970. Regarding this work by Spínola, Marcello Caetano would later state, already in Brazil, that he repented for 'having imprudently placed cavalry officers in spheres of knowledge where they can easily go astray.' Serrão, Joaquim Veríssimo, *Marcelo Caetano – Confidências no Exílio*, (Lisbon: Editorial Verbo, 1985), p.362.

35 In his speech to the meeting of the Legislative Council of Guinea on 16 October 1972, Spínola clearly advocated broad autonomy for the African territories with elective organs and self-government, a speech which did not please Marcello Caetano, nor Silva Cunha, who was Minister of Overseas Territories. Caetano criticised Spínola's proposal for having provisions contrary to the Organic Law of Overseas Territories. Cf. *País sem Rumo*, p.66; pp.376–377. Caetano, Marcello, *O 25 de Abril e o Ultramar. Três entrevistas e alguns documentos*, (Lisbon: Verbo, n.d.), p.100.

36 AHPR – GB/GB0205/1729/056: Exposition of the Governor and Commander-in-Chief of the Armed Forces of Guinea. Meeting of the Supreme Council of National Defence on 7 May 1971. During this meeting of the CSDN, Spínola made a presentation on the situation in Guinea which is attached to the report of the meeting.

37 This is the opinion he expresses to Spínola in a letter dated 22 March 1973. Cf. *O 25 de Abril e o Ultramar. Três entrevistas e alguns documentos*, p.119.

38 MPR/AAS/CX000/0268. Dedication to the President of the Republic, in the book *Portugal e o Futuro*.

39 Thomaz, *Últimas décadas de Portugal*, pp.345–346.

40 Spínola, António de, *Portugal e o Futuro*, 5th Edition, (Lisbon: Arcádia, 1974), pp.42–45.

41 Spínola, *Portugal e o Futuro*, p.234 .

42 *Ibid.*, p.12.

43 *Ibid.*, p . 56.

44 Caetano, *Depoimento*, pp.196–197.

45 Spínola, *País sem rumo*, p.75.

46 Spínola, *País sem rumo*, p.76.

47 Pinto, Pedro Feytor, *Na Sombra do Poder*, (Lisbon: Publicações D. Quixote, 2011), p.250.

48 *Ibid.*, p.251.

49 MPR/AAS/CX000/0269: Letter from Francisco Sá Carneiro to António de Spínola thanking him for the book '*Portugal e o Futuro*,' 4 March 1974.

50 MPR/AAS/CX000/0272: Letter from Adriano Moreira to António de Spínola thanking him for sending the book '*Portugal e o Futuro*' and appreciating its contents.

51 MPR/AAS/CX000/0267: Letter from António Ramalho Eanes to António de Spínola thanking him for the gift of the book '*Portugal e o Futuro*.' Eanes had served in Guinea, during Spínola's time, in the *Repartição de Assuntos Civis e Ação Psicológica do Comando-Chefe*, having been in charge of the Broadcasting and Press Service.

52 *Ibid.*

53 MPR/AAS/CX000/0270: Letter from António de Spínola to António Ramalho Eanes explaining the reasons for writing '*Portugal e o Futuro*,' 19 April 1974.
54 Telegram 778, American Embassy Lisbon to Department of State, March 1, 1974, 'Prestigious Military Leader Calls For Federation Of Lusitanian States,' State Department, National Archives, Washington D.C.
55 Archives du MAE, FR MAE 200QO, Direction Europe, Portugal 1971–1976, Politique intérieure 130, série 28, sous série 3, dossier 1, 1974, Ambassade de France au Portugal, Lettre nº 235, Lisbonne, le 1 mars 1974. Bernard Durand, Ambassadeur de France au Portugal, à son Excellence Monsieur le ministre des Affaires étrangères.
56 Archives du MAE , FR MAE 200QO, Direction Europe, Portugal 1971–1976, Politique intérieure 130, série 28, sous série 3, dossier 1, 1974, Ambassade de France au Portugal, Télégramme n° 59–62, Lisbonne, le 11 mars 1974. Bernard Durand, Ambassador of France in Portugal, to his Excellency, the Minister for Foreign Affairs.
57 Carvalho, *Alvorada em Abril*, p.217.
58 Carvalho, *Alvorada em Abril*, pp.219–222.
59 Spínola, *País sem rumo*, p.91.
60 *Ibid.*, p.378.
61 ADN/GABMIN/007/0035/051: Supreme Military Council. Summary of the meeting of 24 March 1973.
62 In his memoirs, Pereira Crespo says that he made Viana Rebelo see the drawbacks of the proposed measures, but that they had the support of the CEMGFA, General Costa Gomes, which convinced Viana Rebelo of its convenience. Crespo, Manuel Pereira, *Porque Perdemos a Guerra*, (Edições Abril, 1977), pp.115–116.
63 In the National Defence Archive, there is a folder in the CEMGFA collection – ADN/CEMGFA/004/0004/006 – on the movement of the captains, which contains the letter sent from Bissau on 28 August 1973.
64 The two telegrams are in the background already mentioned: ADN/CEMGFA/004/0004/006.
65 ADN/CEMGFA/004/0004/006: DGS information Nos. 38/73-DINF 2 and 45/73-DINF 2.
66 ADN/CEMGFA/004/0005/016. This directive temporarily calmed the QP officers, who saw this as a victory, but aggravated the claims of the militia officers. Cf. Almeida, Dinis de, *Origens e evolução do Movimento de Capitães: subsídios para uma melhor compreensão*, 2nd edition (Lisbon: Ed.Sociais, 1977), p.161.
67 Almeida, *Origens e evolução do Movimento de Capitães*, pp.165–168.
68 In a letter to Joaquim Veríssimo Serrão in 1978, Marcello Caetano explained that the choice of Silva Cunha for National Defence was a suggestion by General Costa Gomes. As for the position of Army Minister, the first choice had been General Silvino Silvério Marques, but he declined the invitation because he could not bear to work with Silva Cunha and because he believed that a civilian should not hold the position of Minister of Defence. Serrão, Joaquim Veríssimo, *Correspondência com Marcello Caetano – 1974–1980*, (Venda Nova: Bertrand Editora, 1994), p.162. This version is confirmed by Santos e Castro, governor of Angola, who learnt from General Luz Cunha, commander-in-chief of the Portuguese forces in Angola, that Costa Gomes would like to see Silva Cunha in the Ministry of Defence and advised Marcello Caetano to do so. Cf. Santos e Castro interview by José Freire Antunes in *A Guerra de África*, Volume II (Lisbon: Círculo de Leitores, 1995), pp.860–861.
69 Lemos, Viana de, *Duas Crises, 1961 e 1974 – um olhar de um oficial do exército português*, 2nd edition, (Lisbon: Edições Cosmos, 2009), pp.68–69.
70 Carvalho, *Alvorada em Abril*, pp.182–183.
71 *Ibid.*, p.189.
72 *Ibid.*, pp.194–195.
73 *Ibid.*, p.198.
74 Spínola, *País sem rumo*, pp.91–93.
75 AMC/PC-UTL: Unsigned handwritten account of the conversation between Marcello Caetano and António Spínola, dated 7 March 1974, Ultramar, Relatórios, Cx 12, no. 10.
76 Cunha, *Ainda o 25 de Abril*, pp.80–81.
77 País sem Rumo p.93.
78 Cunha, *Ainda o 25 de Abril*, p.81.
79 AMC/12-1512: Letter from Vítor Manuel de Aguiar e Silva, Member of Parliament of the National Assembly, dated 24 February 1974, Cx. 54, no. 6.
80 Crespo, *Porque Perdemos a Guerra*, p.132.
81 Pinto, *Na Sombra do Poder*, p.254.
82 Thomaz, *Últimas Décadas de Portugal*, p.348.
83 Kaúlza was one of the personalities of the so-called 'Belém group' that put pressure on Thomaz to replace Marcello Caetano's Government. See Arriaga, Kaúlza de, *Guerra e Política: Em nome da Verdade, Os Anos Decisivos*, 2nd edition, (Lisbon: Edições Referendo, 1987), p.69.
84 Múrias, Manuel Maria, *De Salazar a Costa Gomes*, (Lisbon: Nova Arrancada, 1998), p.284.
85 Telegram 45989, Department of State, March 7, 1974, 'Spínola Call For Self-determination in Portuguese Africa Precipitates Political Crisis,' State Department, National Archives, Washington D.C.
86 Caetano, *Depoimento*, p.197. Jorge Jardim, who was a very influential politician in the former regime, reveals that Américo Thomaz told him in exile that the name Marcello had suggested to lead the new government was Baltazar Rebelo de Sousa, who at the time was Minister of Overseas Territories and very close to Marcello Caetano. Cf. Jardim, Jorge, *Moçambique-Terra Queimada* (Lisbon: Editorial Intervenção, 1976), p.210.
87 *Ibid.*, p.198.

Chapter 2

1 Themido, João Hall, *Dez anos em Washington,1971–1981*, (Lisbon: Dom Quixote, 1995), p.100.
2 Memorandum From the Executive Secretary of the Department of State (Pickering) to the President's Deputy Assistant for National Security Affairs (Scowcroft), Washington, September 18, 1973, Document 123, National Archives, Nixon Presidential Materials, NSC Files, Box 701, Country Files, Europe, Portugal, Vol. II (1972–1974).
3 *Ibid.*
4 *Ibid.* Portugal, Document 124.
5 Themido, *Dez anos em Washington*, pp.113–120.
6 Antunes, José Freire, Os Americanos e Portugal. Nixon e Caetano: Promessas e Abandono 1969–1974, (Lisbon: Difusão Cultural, 1992), p.279. Telegram 203571 From the Department of State to the Embassy in Portugal, *Washington, October 13, 1973, Document 125, Nixon Presidential Materials, NSC Files, Box 701, Country Files, Europe, Portugal, Vol. II (1972–1974).*
7 In 32 days, American aircraft carried 22,000 tons of cargo to Israel flying 566 missions. The Soviets in 40 days carried 15,000 tons of cargo to the Arab allies flying 935 missions, which shows that the American transport force was much more efficient with Lajes playing an important role in refuelling and crew exchange.

Supplies were quickly transported to the front line reaching the northern front with Syria in 3 hours and the Sinai in about 20 hours. Cf. Ulanoff Stanley M. and Eshel, David, *The Fighting Israeli Air Force – The Amazing Combat History of the World's Finest Air Force 1948–1984*, (New York: Arco Publishing, INC, 1985), pp.87–89.

8 AHPR/GB/GB0205/1729/104: Supreme Council of National Defence – Report of the session of 19 October 1973.

9 Letter From Portuguese Prime Minister Caetano to President Nixon, Lisbon, October 19, 1973, Document 127, Nixon Presidential Materials, NSC Files, Box 701, Country Files, Europe, Portugal, Vol. II (1972–1974).

10 The *Redeye* was an individual infrared guided missile that could be fired from the shoulder. The missile could reach up to 4,500 metres and due to its mobility was ideal to protect the Portuguese troops in Guinea who were widely dispersed throughout the colony. See ADN/SGDN/1REP/177/0711/021: US Army Manual on the Redeye.

11 *Ibid.*

12 It should be noted that at that time the negotiations with the French for the purchase of Crotale anti-aircraft missiles were well under way. The manufacturer of the missile, Thomson-CSF, was in contact with General Costa Gomes, through a Portuguese company, Sociedade Comercial Romar, in order to close a contract for the purchase of this type of equipment. Cf. ADN/SGDN/3REP/238/0738/041.

13 AHPR/GB/GB0205/1729/104: Higher Council of National Defence – Report of the session of 19 October 1973.

14 At this meeting, the Minister of Finance, Cota Dias, announced that the funds intended for the re-equipment of the armed forces for the following three years (1974/76) amounted to four and a half billion escudos. Cf. AHPR/GB/GB0205/1729/104.

15 ADN/CEMGFA/014/0029/005: Telegram from the Portuguese Embassy in Washington, 27 November 1973.

16 ADN/CEMGFA/014/0029/005: Telegram from DELNATO from Portugal in Brussels. Memo from the Ministry of Foreign Affairs on the Minister's conversation with the American Secretary of State, Dr. Kissinger on December 9, 1973, Lisbon, 10 December 1973. See also memorandum on the conversation in Brussels between Rui Patrício and Kissinger in Richard M. Nixon National Security Files, 1969–1974, Western Europe. https://history.state.gov/historicaldocuments/frus1969-76ve15p2/d130

17 Israel had in fact had Hawk missiles since 1962. Cf. Tal, David, *Symbol Not Substance? Israel's Campaign to Acquire Hawk Missiles, 1960–1962*, The International History Review
Vol. 22, No. 2 (Jun. 2000), pp.304–317.

18 ADN/CEMGFA/014/0029/005: Telegram from the Portuguese Embassy in Washington to the Ministry of Foreign Affairs, 11 December 1973.

19 Overseas air defence requirements led Portugal to request a Raytheon HAWK (Homing All-the-Way Killer) missile battery from the US in 1973–74. The issue was raised repeatedly during negotiations over continued American use of the Lajes air base, but Washington consistently equivocated, citing political obstacles.

20 ADN/CEMGFA/014/0029/005: Telegram to the Portuguese Embassy in Washington, 13 December 1973. It is assumed that the Portuguese interest would be in having wheeled vehicles, where it would be possible to mount a system to fire the BGM-71 TOW, an anti-tank missile used by the American forces.

21 ADN/CEMGFA/014/0029/005: Telegram from the Portuguese Embassy in Washington to the Ministry of Foreign Affairs, 13 December 1973.

22 ADN/CEMGFA/014/0029/005: Telegram from the Ministry of Foreign Affairs to the Portuguese Embassy in Washington, 14 December 1973.

23 ADN/CEMGFA/014/0029/005: Telegram from the Portuguese Embassy in Washington to the Ministry of Foreign Affairs, 15 December 1973.

24 ADN/CEMGFA/014/0029/005: Pro memoria. The Açores Agreement.

25 This reference seems to relate to a failed attempt in Italy to shoot down an Israeli commercial airliner with SA-7 missiles in September 1973 by PLO members of the Black September group.

26 *Foreign Relations of the United States*, 1969–1976, Volume E–15, Part 2, Documents on Western Europe, 1973–1976, second revised edition, ed. Kathleen B. Rasmussen (Washington: Government Publishing Office, 2021), Portugal, Document 130.

27 AHD/3/MNE-SE-GMS/GM/081/000014: Visit of Dr. Henry Kissinger to Portugal, 1973.

28 AMC/PC/02: Negotiations with the US on the Azores – 1973–1974. Cx 12, No. 34.

29 Telegram 173, American Embassy Lisbon to Department of State, January 15, 1974, 'Foreign Minister Desire For Response From Secretary,' State Department, National Archives, Washington D.C.

30 ADN/CEMGFA/014/0029/005: Telegram from the Portuguese Embassy in Washington to the Ministry of Foreign Affairs, 8 February 1974.

31 ADN/CEMGFA/014/0029/005: Letter from Ministry of Foreign Affairs (Cabinet Min.) to Henry Kissinger, 7 March 1974.

32 Themido, *op. cit.*

33 The statement Themido carried effectively proposed an end to American facilities at Lajes, 'which in the present circumstances of world politics no longer have the justification they had in the past.' Any future request to grant new facilities would be examined on a case-by-case basis. See ADN/CEMGFA/014/0029/005.

34 ADN/CEMGFA/014/0029/005: Letter from the Ambassador in Washington on the negotiations for the renewal of the Azores Agreement – Session of 18 March 1974. See also: Telegram 54891, Department of State to American Embassy Lisbon, March 19, 1974, 'Azores negotiations,' State Department, National Archives, Washington.

35 ADN/CEMGFA/014/0029/005: Letter from the Ambassador in Washington, No.287 – Proc.15–21 to the Minister of Foreign Affairs, 20 March 1974.

36 ADN/CEMGFA/014/0029/005: Letter from Henry Kissinger to the Minister of Foreign Affairs, 11 April 1974.

37 ADN – Fundo Geral Cx. 833/9: Note no. 1229/AF/74 from the General Staff of the Armed Forces to the Director General of Public Accounting, Subject: Purchase of 'REDEYE' missile-launcher-kits (31–7–1974). We have information from a telegram of the American Embassy in Lisbon that each missile cost 14,000 US dollars for an order of 1,000 units and that the delivery time was 30 months. Given the speed with which the missiles were obtained they could only have come from the Israeli arsenal. Cf. Telegram 877, American Embassy Lisbon to Department of State, March 8, 1974, 'Redeye Weapon System (U)', State Department, National Archives, Washington D.C.

38 ADN/SGDN/1REP/177/0718/048: Information no. 173/RA, SGDN proc. 822.60 of 19 July 1974. Subject: Redeye surface-to-air missiles.

39 ADN/SGDN/1REP/177/0718/048: Information no. 173/RA, SGDN proc. 822.60 of 19 July 1974. Subject: Redeye surface-to-air missiles.

40 ADN/CEMGFA/014/0029/005: Note (annexed to letter PEA-173) with the programme for the realisation of the first nuclear power plant and tables 1 and 2 annexed to it, 22 April 1974.

41 ADN/CEMGFA/014/0029/005: Letter from the Minister of Foreign Affairs (Cabinet) – PEA-713, 23 April 1974.

Chapter 3

1 ADN/SGDN/2REP/206/0722/040: report of the incidents that occurred on 17JAN74; Carvalho, *Alvorada em Abril*, pp.189–190.

2 Carvalho, *op. cit.* , p.196.

3 ADN/SGDN/1REP/079/0279/024: Report of the visit of CEMGFA to Mozambique and its annexes, January 1974.

4 Jardim, *Moçambique – Terra Queimada*, p.165.

5 *Ibid.*, p.165.

6 Records of the working meeting with the various members of the government. *op. cit.*

7 *Ibid.*, pp.24–26.

8 *Ibid.*, pp.36–39.

9 ADN/CEMGFA/032/0068/001: (Memorandum) Delineation of Study No. 07831/CG, p. 0022, dated 19 March 1973.

10 ADN/CEMGFA/030/0066/010: Remarks by General CEMGFA on his arrival in Lisbon.

11 ADN/SGDN/1REP/079/0280/03: Letter to General Costa Gomes signed by João Soares Cabeçadas, n.d.

12 ADN/SGDN/1REP/079/0279/024: Report of CEMGFA's Visit to Mozambique, Annex D, Appendix 1, RMM. HQ. 3rd Rep.

13 *Ibid.*, Report of CEMGFA's Visit to Mozambique, pp.11–15.

14 *Ibid.*, p.16.

15 ADN/CEMGFA/032/0068/002: Personal letter to the Commander of Mozambique, no. 05243/GC/32/S, p.2511, from CEMGFA. Lisbon, 20 February 1974.

16 *Ibid.*, Opinion no. 06645/GC of 7 March 1974 from CEMGFA. Subject: Displacement of the HQ/CCFAM. See also: CEMGFA Opinion no. 07147/GC, p.2635, dated 12 March 1974. Subject: Displacement of the HQ/CCFAM.

17 Swift, Kerry, *Mozambique and the future*, (Cape Town: Don Nelson, 1974), pp.129–130.

18 One of the Rhodesian officers who participated in this operation, Petter-Bowyer, gives a detailed account of it in his book *Winds of Destruction* (Pinetown: 30th South Publishers, 2005), pp.222–227.

19 Cardoso, José Armando Vizela, *Voando no céu do reino de Monomotapa. Guerra do Ultramar. Moçambique 1972–1974*, (Porto: Fronteira do Caos, 2016), pp.273–279.

20 In an interview with the South African journalist Kerry Swift, in 1974, the commander of the Portuguese Air Force in Mozambique, General Diogo Neto, had already foreseen the arrival of the missile in that territory. Swift, *op. cit.*, p.133.

21 On 13 February, the 3rd Air Region Command in Mozambique issued a situation study in which it defined all the procedures that should be adopted to mitigate the missile threat. Cardoso, *op. cit.*, pp.393–403.

22 Swift, *op. cit.*, pp.132–135.

23 ADN/SGDN/2REP/206/0720/017: Msg. no. 140 of 11 April 1974 from the General Government of Mozambique to the Ministry of Overseas Territories.

24 Caetano, *O 25 de Abril e o Ultramar* , p.103.

25 Tavares-Teles, António, *Otelo – 18 de Janeiro*, (Lisbon: Author's Edition, 1976), p.304.

26 ADN/CEMGFA/017/0034/009: Letter from ZACVG Commander to CEMGFA, Bissau, 27 November 1973.

27 ADN/CEMGFA/010/0023/037: Supreme Defence Council, 2nd vol.

28 Spínola, *País sem Rumo*, pp.54–58. In his memoirs, Silva Cunha admits that when the letter arrived in Lisbon, there was great alarm and that it was decided to send General Costa Gomes to Guinea to gather more information. Cf. Cunha, *O Ultramar, a Nação e o 25 de Abril*, p.53.

29 Spínola, *op. cit.*

30 AHM/DIV/2/04/316/04: Memorandum from the Chief of Staff of CEMGFA dated 28 May 1973.

31 AHM/FO/029/15/370/11: Commander-in-Chief of the Guinean Armed Forces – Records of the command meeting of 8 June 1973. In his analysis, Lieutenant-Colonel Beirão stated that there was information that the Republic of Guinea had eight MiG-17 and six MiG-19 fighters, and that the PAIGC also had six planes, four of which were reconnaissance planes. The MiG fighters were said to be piloted by Libyan and Algerian pilots. We now know that this information was exaggerated. The only existing fighter jet in the neighbouring country was the MiG-17 and the PAIGC had no aircraft at all. The MiG fighters were flown by Cuban and Guinean pilots. Cf. Hernandez, Humberto C. Trujillo, *El Grito del Baobab*, (Habana: Editorial de Ciencias Sociales, 2008).

32 Spínola, *País sem rumo*, p.62. During the visit, Silva Cunha recognised that there was a different state of mind in the officers with whom he had contact in relation to previous visits, noting less cordiality. Cf. Cunha, *O Ultramar, a Nação e o 25 de Abril*, p.55.

33 There is some disagreement regarding the participants in this meeting. In his memoirs, Silva Cunha, mentions the presence of the ministers of Defence, Navy, Foreign Affairs, Overseas, besides Costa Gomes. Cunha, op. cit. Marcello Caetano, probably by oversight, makes no reference to the minister of Foreign Affairs.

34 The records of this meeting were destroyed after 25 April 1974, but the handwritten notes of the secretary of the CSDN have been located in the Archives of the Presidency of the Republic. Although they are not complete, they allow us to see much of what was discussed at the meeting.

35 ADN/SGDN/2REP/106/0417/031: Survey of enemy air assets and neighbouring countries by Guinea Chief Command, Bissau, 10 November 1973. This fear was exaggerated, given that the Soviets were unlikely to provide combat jets to the PAIGC and the MiGs that were in Conakry flew little despite the Cuban assistance they had, but the Portuguese had little information about the neighbouring country's true air capabilities.

36 Cunha, *O Ultramar, a Nação e o 25 de Abril* , p.54.

37 Caetano, *Depoimento*, p.180.

38 Caetano, op. cit. In an interview with Maria Manuela Cruzeiro, Costa Gomes says that the first choice for Guinea was General Diogo Neto, who was in Mozambique as commander of the Air Force. However, Diogo Neto refused the invitation alleging that he had no administrative experience for the functions of governor which he would accumulate with those of military command. Bettencourt Rodrigues was thus a second choice and only accepted the post due to his friendship with Marcello Caetano. Cf. Cruzeiro, *Costa Gomes: O ultimo marechal, p.169*.

39 These two companies were to take over from CCaç 3407 and 3408 in Angola, which returned to the mainland without having been replaced, leaving the command of the Angolan Armed Forces dissatisfied with the situation. (Note no. 1824RO, of 9 August 73, CCFAA. Cf. ADN/CEMGFA/019/0039/008).

40 AHD – PAA 960, 18 Packet 1140. Lists attached to the letter from the Portuguese Minister of Defence to the South African Minister of Defence, January 1973. See also ADN/CEMGFA/025/0058/021: List of materials to be submitted to the RSA, 19 July 1972. In the documents of the Alcora High Level Commission (ATLC), consultable at ADN/CCAU/001/0003/014, it is possible to see several lists of materiel submitted to South Africa in June 1972 and corrected in June 1973 by the Angola Military Region, and other issues related to Pretoria's military assistance.

41 ADN/GABMIN/007/0038/072: Letter from the Ministry of Foreign Affairs to the Chief of Staff of the Minister of National Defence, 28 May 1973.

42 AHD – PAA 960, 18 Packet 1140: Telegram no. 262 from the Portuguese Embassy in Pretoria, 30 August 1973.

43 AHD – PAA 960, 18 Packet 1140: Telegram No. 363 from the Portuguese Embassy in Pretoria, 11 December 1973. See also memorial of the General Staff of the Armed Forces, 18 September 1975. We can see from the correspondence that the negotiations were difficult regarding the final value of the loan and that it was only at the end of 1973 that the South Africans agreed to the 150 million rands. See also correspondence in ADN/GABMIN/007/0038/072.

44 Miller, J., Things fall apart: South Africa and the collapse of the Portuguese Empire, 1973–74. *Cold War History*, 12:2, 2012, pp.183–204.

45 Rocha, João Manuel, *Guiné-Bissau – Os camaradas estão a perguntar se é assim que se toma a independência*, (Guinea-Bissau – Comrades are asking if this is how to take Independence), *Público* newspaper, 24 September 2013.

46 ADN/CEMGFA/015/0032/041: Supreme Defence Council: information. Situation in the Period OCT73 to JAN74, TO GUINEA. Enemy Activities Abroad, p.5.

47 ADN/GABMIN/007/0038/072: Note from the Ministry of Foreign Affairs on the problem of Portuguese participation in international meetings attended by delegates from the so-called 'Independent Republic of Guinea-Bissau,' 27 November 1973.

48 Archives du MAE, FR MAE 200QO , Guinea-Bissau: indépendance et reconnaissance internationale, 199, Janvier-juillet 1974 , Lettre de Senghor à Olof Palme, 26 décembre 1973.

49 Archives du MAE, FR MAE 200QO, Guinée-Bissau: indépendance et reconnaissance internationale, 199, Janvier-juillet 1974 , ministre de l'Enseignement supérieur, Note à l'attention du Président de la République, Dakar, 13 janvier 1974.

50 Archives du MAE, FR MAE 200QO, Guinée-Bissau: indépendance et reconnaissance internationale, 199, Janvier-juillet 1974, Télégramme de l'ambassadeur de France au Sénégal, Dakar, le 20 février 1974.

51 Archives du MAE, FR MAE 200QO, Guinée-Bissau: indépendance et reconnaissance internationale, 199, Janvier-juillet 1974, Direction des Affaires Africaines et Malgaches, note pour le cabinet du ministre, Paris, le 4 mars 1974.

52 ADN/GABMIN/007/0029/007: Letter from the Commander-in-Chief of the Guinean Armed Forces to the Minister for Overseas Territories, Subject: Journalist visits to Boé, 20 November 1973. See also messages and correspondence from the Guinea Governor's Office about visits of journalists to Boé in ADN/CEMGFA/017/0037/063 and also visit of journalists to Boé with photos: ADN/SGDN/2REP/074/0320/017.

53 ADN/CEMGFA/017/0034/004: Summary of the study of the CCFAG on the Boé area, General Secretariat of National Defence, File No. 2202, Folder A, (n.d.)

54 Caio, Horácio, Guiné 74 – Vigilância e Resposta, (Lisbon: 1974), p.31. See also RTP Archives – Visita do Ministro do Ultramar às colônias da Guiné-Bissau e Cabo Verde: https://arquivos.rtp.pt/conteudos/visita-do-ministro-do-ultramar-as-colonias/

55 Caio, *op. cit.*, p.49. RTP archives: https://arquivos.rtp.pt/conteudos/visita-do-ministro-do-ultramar-a-guine-bissau/

56 ADN/CEMGFA/015/0032/041: Supreme Defence Council: information. Situation from OCT73 to JAN74, TO GUINEA, p.9. See also 'Plane shot down by surface-to-air missile in January 1974,' ADN/SGDN/2REP/074/0320/026.

57 The attack is carried out by PAIGC commander Mamadu Cassamá, who eventually died from a landmine.

58 Interviews with António Rodrigues and João Ribeiro in *A Guerra* de Joaquim Furtado, episode 41, 2013.

59 ADN/GABMIN/007/0038/077: Information No 355 from the Secretary of State for Aeronautics, Subject: Strela (TRACOR) anti-missile equipment, 18 April 1974.

60 ADN/FDMU/045/0115/026: Information no. 384/AF/74 from SGDN, Subject: Anti-missile measures 'Strella' – procurement in RSA of anti-missile equipment for helicopters, 20 May 1974. The charge for the acquisition of this equipment for helicopters was to be supported by the South African loan. The acquisition of 176 devices was foreseen.

61 ADN/SGDN/1REP/061/0225/024: an information from the 4th Division/EMGFA of 22 October 1974 about the night vision devices from Rank Precision Industries, reports that the purchase was authorised in May 1974 and that the devices were to be distributed to the theatres of operations in Guinea, Angola, and Mozambique.

62 Folques, Raul, 'Os Comandos na Guiné,' *Revista 'Mama Sume,'* No. 64, 2006, pp.13–20.

63 ADN/SGDN/1REP/062/0233/006: Monthly summary of operational activity overseas. For March 74. Guinea TO.

64 Since August 1973, the military command in Bissau had information about the possible use of toxic smoke grenades by the PAIGC. However, it was never possible to confirm the use of this type of grenades or toxic gases by the guerrillas. Cf. ADN/SGDN/2REP/106/0421/042 and ADN/SGDN/2REP/078/0329/007.

65 Interview with Bettencourt Rodrigues in *A Guerra* (The War) of Joaquim Furtado, episode 17, 2013.

66 ADN/SGDN/2REP/078/0329/007: Device Remodelling in the Eastern Zone, HQ/CCFAG, Bissau, 19 March 1974.

67 AHM/DIV/2/4/223/004: Report of the 2nd Division of the Guinea Territorial Independent Command, (1975).

68 ADN/SGDN/2REP/088/0364/02: Chief Command of the Guinean Armed Forces to SGDN, Subject: update of SUPINTREP No. 33 (Enemy armament and equipment). Armoured Fighting Vehicles – General, Bissau, 17 May 1974. Today we know from photos of the time that they were BRDM-2 vehicles.

69 ADN/CEMGFA/005/0011/022: Correspondence between General Costa Gomes and General Emílio Villaescusa Quilis (1974).

70 ADN/CEMGFA/017/0034/009: Report of the CCFAG, 12 March 1974. Besides the military difficulties, Bettencourt Rodrigues also complained to Costa Gomes about the lack of funds for the social part, not being able to have the same funds that Spínola had in this field. Cf. Cruzeiro, *Costa Gomes: O último marechal*, pp.169–170.

71 ADN/SGDN/3REP/238/0737/037: Report of the military mission abroad from 5 to 16 January 1974 (Israel).

72 ADN/GABMIN/007/0035/051: Memorandum of 30 May 1973 from the Secretary of State for Aeronautics to the Minister for National Defence, Subject: Aircraft Fleet Renewal.

73 Portugal ended up buying 28 Aviocar and 32 Milirole aircraft.
74 The FNLA would be created in 1962, when the UPA joined the Democratic Party of Angola (PDA).
75 ADN/CEMGFA/015/0032/041: Supreme Defence Council: information. Situation from OCT73 to JAN74, ANGOLA.
76 ADN/CEMGFA/019/0039/008: Exposition of the General Commander-in-Chief of the Angolan Armed Forces, Subject: Situation in Cabinda and Northern Angola. Meeting on 30 January 1974.
77 ADN/SGDN/1REP/042/0144/004: Note No. 1415 from the Commander-in-Chief of the Angolan Armed Forces to the Chief of the General Staff of the Armed Forces, Subject: Evolution of the military situation in Cabinda – Set of operational measures taken, Luanda, 19 April 1974.
78 ADN/SGDN/1REP/042/0144/004: Letter from the Minister of Defence of the Republic of South Africa to the Minister of National Defence, Lisbon, 11 March 1974.
79 ADN/SGDN/1REP/042/0144/004: Annex 1 to the records of 20ABR74 under Operation Stop.
80 ADN/SGDN/1REP/040/0138/006: Notes on the loan of Impala aircraft under Operation Victor, 1969.
81 ADN/SGDN/1REP/040/0137/004: Talks on ceding materials by South Africa, aircraft, 1969.

Chapter 4

1 AHM/FO/007/A/19: Office of the Chief of Staff of the Army (CEME) – Reports on subversion, 1967–1974, Cx. 40, no. 8, 1974.
2 AMC/12-721: Correspondence, Francisco Vale Guimarães, Cx. 28, no. 19.
3 AMC/12-154: Correspondence, Mário Bacelar Begonha, Cx. 17, no. 4.
4 Statement by Miguel Caetano to Zélia Oliveira, 2012.
5 Carvalho, *Alvorada em Abril*, pp.223–224.
6 *Ibid.*, pp.224–225.
7 AHM/FO/006/I/14: Office of the Minister of the Army, Cx. 484, no. 24 – Press releases and broadcasting of military news by the daily press, radio and television, 1974.
8 AMC/12-809: Records of the meeting of 4 March 1974, Office of the Secretary of State for the Army, Cx. 33, no. 2.
9 AMC/PC/05: Speeches and interviews 1972–1974, Cx. 13, no. 13, speech of 5 March 1974 before the National Assembly. See also *Diário de Notícias* newspaper of 6 March 1974. According to Silva Cunha, on the eve of the speech, Caetano summoned some ministers more concerned with political, military, and overseas problems to inform them of the speech and ask for their opinion. This meeting is confirmed by the Minister of the Navy, Pereira Crespo, who was present. Strangely Silva Cunha was not summoned to this meeting, which led the Minister of Defence, the following day, to present his resignation to the head of the government. Caetano did not accept the resignation and reiterated his confidence in the minister, explaining to him that he had not summoned him so as not to compromise him with the statements he was going to make in the National Assembly, which made Silva Cunha even more suspicious, as he did not understand how he (the minister) could not agree with what was going to be said. Cf. Cunha, *Ainda o 25 de Abril*, p.110. Marcello Caetano's speech is reproduced in his book *Depoimento*, pp.222–237. The speech can be seen online on Portuguese TV: https://arquivos.rtp.pt/conteudos/discurso-de-marcelo-caetano-3/
10 Caetano, *Depoimento*, pp.222–237.
11 Carvalho, *Alvorada em Abril*, pp.225–226.
12 Crespo, *Porque Perdemos a Guerra*, p.134.
13 Caetano, *op. cit.* p.199.
14 Official Gazette, no. 108, Legislative Session 2, X Legislature, p.2078.
15 Thomaz, *op. cit.* p.349.
16 AMC/12-1363: José Eduardo Tavares Rodrigues, Letter, 22 February 1974, Correspondence/Rodrigues, Cx. 48, no. 70.
17 AMC/12-1375, Álvaro Luís de Roure Roquette, Letter of 12-03-1974, Correspondence/Roquete, Cx. 49, no. 1.
18 Caetano, *op. cit.*, p.199.
19 Carvalho, *op. cit.*, pp.229–237.
20 There is some controversy regarding the way Costa Gomes and Spínola were chosen. Vasco Lourenço, in an interview with Maria Manuela Cruzeiro, reports that there was a vote and that Costa Gomes won by a large majority. Cf. Cruzeiro, *Vasco Lourenço, do Interior da Revolução*, pp.170–171. In an interview with Manuel Bernardo, Captain Vergílio Varela argues that the vote was a show of hands and that the two generals were chosen together without distinction as to the vote. Cf. Bernardo, Manuel, *Marcello e Spínola: A Ruptura. As Forças Armadas e a Imprensa na Queda do Estado Novo, 1973–1974*, (Lisbon: Edições Margem, 1994), p.394.
21 On this issue, Vergílio Varela, in an interview with Manuel Bernardo, says that Costa Gomes was aware of the MFA programme and gave his approval without proposing any changes. Cf. Bernardo, *op. cit.*, p.394.
22 Cruzeiro, *op. cit.*, p.181.
23 *Ibid.*, p.203.
24 *Ibid.*, p.219.
25 Cruzeiro, *Vasco Lourenço do Interior da Revolução*, pp.169–170.
26 Spínola, *op. cit.*, pp.94–95.
27 CRUZEIRO, Maria Manuela, *Melo Antunes, O sonhador pragmático*, 3rd edition, (Lisbon: Editorial de Notícias, 2005), p.61 and pp.71–72.
28 AMC/PC-UTL/01: President of the Council – *Overseas/* Reports, notes, and correspondence – 1968–1974, Note on the meeting, which took place on 7 March 1974, Cx. 12, no. 10. There is also a partial account of this conversation in Marcello Caetano's book, *O 25 de Abril e o Ultramar – Três entrevistas e alguns documentos*, pp.125–128.
29 AMC/PC-UTL/01: Information from the Mozambique Delegation of the DGS on the repercussions of the book *Portugal e o Futuro on* public opinion. Presidente do Conselho, Ultramar/Relatórios notas e correspondência, 1968–1974, Cx. 12, no. 13, Annex 1.
30 AMC/PC-UTL/01: Letter from Luís C. Lupi to Prof. Marcello Caetano with three attached articles, President of the Council, Ultramar/Reports notes and correspondence, 1968–1974, Cx. 12, no. 12, Annexes 1, 2 and 3.
31 'Les Portugais prennent peur,' *L'Express Afrique*, 11 February 1974.
32 Cruzeiro, *Melo Antunes, O Sonhador Pragmático*, pp.54–55.
33 Cruzeiro, *Vasco Lourenço do Interior da Revolução*, pp.166–169.
34 Carvalho, *op.* cit., pp.238–239.
35 *Ibid.*, p.240.
36 Cruzeiro, *Vasco Lourenço do Interior da Revolução*, pp.176–178.
37 Lemos, *Duas crises, 1961 and 1974*, p.76.
38 *Ibid.*, p.78.
39 Carvalho *op.* cit., pp.240–241; Cruzeiro, *Vasco Lourenço do Interior da Revolução*, p.180.
40 Lemos, *op. cit.*, pp.78–79.
41 Cruzeiro, *Vasco Lourenço do Interior da Revolução*, pp.181–187. Regarding Pinto Soares, Viana de Lemos says in his memoirs that he went back to hospital, as he was ill due to psychiatric problems. A few days later he was submitted to the evaluation of a medical

board that recommended his passage to the reserve for psychiatric reasons. Cf. Lemos, p.79. This version does not coincide with that of Pinto Soares, who claims that he was imprisoned until the end of March and then returned home, with his trial scheduled for 28 April at the Supreme Military Court. With the 25 April Revolution, the trial was cancelled, and Pinto Soares was reinstated in the army. Pinto Soares' testimony in the magazine *O Referencial* no. 149, April–June 2023, pp.179–180.

42 Testimony by David Martelo in *O Referencial* no. 149, April–June 2023, pp.124–126.

43 Loudon, Bruce, 'Portuguese Cabinet shake-up likely in bid to defuse army crisis,' The Financial Times, March 13, 1974 , p.6.

ABOUT THE AUTHORS

José Augusto Matos is an independent researcher in military history in Portugal with primary interest in operations of the Portuguese Air Force during colonial wars in Africa, especially in Guinea. He is a regular contributor to numerous European magazines on military aviation and naval subjects, and collaborated in the major project The Air Force at the End of the Empire, published in 2018. He recently wrote with Zélia Oliveira *Rumo à Revolução*, a history of Portugal leading up to the April 1974 overthrow of the *Estado Novo* regime. This is his eighth book for Helion.

Zélia Oliveira is a journalist at the Portuguese National News Agency (Lusa) and holds a master's degree in contemporary Portuguese history. This is his first book for Helion.